A Wiser
Politics

A Wiser Politics

Jean Hardy

EARTH
BOOKS

Winchester, UK
Washington, USA

First published by O-Books, 2011
O-Books is an imprint of John Hunt Publishing Ltd., Laurel House, Station Approach,
Alresford, Hants, SO24 9JH, UK
office1@o-books.net
www.o-books.com

For distributor details and how to order please visit the 'Ordering' section on our website.

Text copyright: Jean Hardy 2010

ISBN: 978 1 84694 567 0

A CIP catalogue record for this book is available from the British Library.

Design: Stuart Davies

Front cover picture: Angela Fahey: Summer Shadows

Printed in the UK by CPI Antony Rowe
Printed in the USA by Offset Paperback Mfrs, Inc

We operate a distinctive and ethical publishing philosophy in all
areas of our business, from our global network of authors to
production and worldwide distribution.

CONTENTS

Dedication

to Jack Hardy, my father,
1908-1944
who died as a prisoner of war

**

Acknowledgements

my most heartfelt thanks are to the 1944 Education Act, which opened so many doors in my life, to a huge variety of people, and to amazing organizations, so that I can just go on learning with curiosity....

the particular organizations are:- the Nottingham Girls High School: the Universities of London, Birmingham and Brunel: Devon County Council Childrens Department: the Psychosynthesis and Education Trust: the Society of Friends (Quakers): the Scientific and Medical Network: St James Church, Piccadilly: Greenspirit: Dartington Hall: and Schumacher College in Devon, including the Tuesday Group

the people who have particularly helped with this book are Wendy Stayte, Thalia Vitali, Chris Marsh, Alan Gibson, Stella Rimington, Jean Boulton, Satish Kumar, Marian McCain, Ann Rimmer, David Lorimer, Susan Hannis, Ruth and Kit Carson,

and to the Devon countryside

Introduction

It is truly remarkable that in the intense political discussions that take place daily and energetically, there is little overt awareness of the deeper philosophy and values of the political parties. Liberal Democrats do not look back to the long history of liberalism and democracy in Europe to appeal to the electorate. Socialists do not mention the six-hundred year fight for equality between rich and poor, men and women, in this society or feel obliged to apologise for the fact that differences in wealth have increased in the thirteen years of their time in power. Conservatives are the most likely to feel their deep psychological and social adherence to competition, class and capitalism, but by and large prefer not to argue for these values, just to live them out. Indeed most political discourse and persuasion is on a far more pragmatic and managerial level, about policies on housing, education, foreign policy, immigration. It is very short-term: whereas, with the issues facing the world, we need to be thinking 'unto the seventh generation', as some older cultures did.

Where is the wider vision? Can we ever truly change our policies unless we can see our present system from a different more comprehensive, and more spiritual, level? Most societies that have ever existed have a social vision which begins with a story about the universe and the earth: an over-arching story which gives a meaning to the whole. But in ours, there is an extraordinary cultural and philosophical gap between everyday life, including politics, and a feeling for and relation to the earth, the universe and our human part in the whole.

I would therefore like to argue in this book for a way of thinking and feeling that links, as many earlier societies have done, Cosmos (a feeling for the Universe and the Earth), with Polis (the early Greek word for the political and social world, then rooted in a participatory democracy), and also Psyche (the vexed but essential question of who we are as human beings). Such a perspective provides a realistic way into the nature of the politics we could pursue if we really wanted a wiser world: we desperately need such a vision. It is well known that you cannot solve problems at the same level as they occur.

* * *

The origins of this book began really early in my life. I was born in the 1930s to a working-class family in Nottingham, England. My father died in the 1939-45 war as a Japanese prisoner of war: my mother throughout the time of the War ran a Trade Union office. But the Education Act of 1944 meant that when my sister Ann and I passed the 11+ exam, we were able to go to the excellent Nottingham Girls High School. I subsequently took my first degree at Bedford College, London University, trained and worked for six years as a social worker, then spent the rest of my fulltime career as a University teacher.

The intellectual origins of this book, and other books I have written, came early in that time. I remember walking to my Junior School in the war through the council estate where we lived, thinking: "I wasn't expecting it to be like this". I must have been about seven. The world was full of men fighting and killing each other: my well-loved father had gone: many of the people around lived very harsh lives, and I suppose we did too. It seemed a rather disastrous place to have arrived – just as it must be so for many children in war-torn places today. The interesting thing, however, is that I seemed to have come expecting something different and enormously much better – what had gone wrong? Where did the expectation that things should be better come from? Wordsworth's "shades of the prison-house" had become obvious to me very early after the beginning of the war, but I also seemed to have a faint recollection of "trailing clouds of glory".

I have always been quite political. My father and mother had both worked for the Nottingham Cooperative Society, and I have always regarded myself as a socialist.

I studied political philosophy in my Sociology degree, attended classes at the London School of Economics. But it wasn't until I was teaching in the Politics and Government Department at Brunel University thirty years later, that I began to develop the ideas basic to this book. I had studied quite a lot of psychology by this time: but what came as a gift when I was in my mid-forties, was finding the Psychosynthesis and Education Trust and their picture of human nature that spoke directly to me, as true. This picture was a dynamic one, quite like Jungian thinking, and contained a sense of spirit, of the clouds of glory I could still at times feel, and which has grown stronger. These two very separate disciplines, the political thought and the psychosynthesis vision, I had to keep quite separate at this time. I wrote my second book, *A Psychology with a Soul* originally in Ph.D. form and it was published in 1987: this book sells pretty well to this day, and has been in five languages.

I left Brunel in 1989, and eventually came to live in South Devon in 1997. I wrote and did all the research work for this politics book in 1993, and put it in a very large red box-file. Life then intervened: one important part of it was attending the ecological and holistic science teaching at Schumacher College, Dartington, and being deeply involved at Dartington Hall, which had been a most creative and beautiful intentional community, and is now a charity, inspiring music, the arts, education and the means for community living. Schumacher College has been a great opportunity for learning, this time about the community of the earth and all her creatures: the College is a living example of the way we all share the same planet and can contemplate the whole universe.

After a startling illness last year, I took out the red file I had put away in 1993, weaving all the learning of the last sixteen years into it, and started to write this book.

* * *

The book is in three sections. The first Part is on our present political myths and philosophies as they have developed since the beginning of the modern European era in the sixteenth century, bringing out the dialogues over the centuries: these stories have come to dominate the modern world. The first chapter is on the importance of stories, myths, and the ways these can become self-fulfilling prophecies. I am not intending to give any kind of definitive overview of the political views of the writers, but rather to weave a thread through the centuries of their philosophical values, around order and change, equality and freedom, government and economics, power and revolution.

The second Part is concerned with the five major elements, concerning the Others, which are omitted, in my view, from this dialogue. The first of these is the female and the feminine – to this day politics is a very male game, not only in terms of persons but also in values. The second is the longstanding, and indigenous, wisdom contained in the history of the human race which modern thinkers have tended to dismiss. The third amazing omission is the Earth and all her creatures who share this place with us – politics has developed as though we lived in a totally human Bubble, and this, I am sure, is the cause of many of our present serious problems. The sense of the spiritual, the mystery, the universe, no longer holds our politics in a framework of wholeness, and this is the fourth omission. And finally, and fifthly, modern politics started from what were concepts of human nature: questioning these concepts is no longer much discussed, even though 'the person', including the child, has been much studied in present times: however our new insights and this understanding has not been applied at all to political thought.

The function of the Third Part is to bring all these diverse and yet deeply related factors together, to begin to put words to a renewed approach to politics, which would include the conscious as well as the unconscious, the golden as well as the dark elements in the stories, and some thought about the problematic future. This bears upon the way we presently divide knowledge into 'disciplines' in schools and in universities, so that it is difficult to relate political thought to science, or economics, or to poetry, in our present system. This division hopefully will soon begin to evaporate, as the problems faced by our world urgently need a synthesis and width of understanding on many levels.

I would like to finish this Introduction with a note on my use of poetry in the book. As a lifelong reader of poetry and novels, I hold that poetry can often get right through to the essence of feeling and intuition around an experience, that prose can rarely reach. I want to present a reasoned book, but also an intuitive and feeling one. This is my way of including another aspect of the Other.

Chapter One

Myths, political myths and self-fulfilling prophecies

The gods did not reveal, from the beginning,
All things to us; but in the course of time,
Through seeking we may learn, and know things better.

But as for certain truth, no man has known it,
Nor will he know it; neither of the gods,
Nor yet of all things of which I speak.
And even if by chance he were to utter
The final truth, he would himself not know it;
For all is but a woven web of guesses.

Xenophanes. (430-350 BCE aprox.)

We have to live by stories, all provisional truths though we work hard to make them more certain. We have nothing else. As Louise Young says in her thoughtful book, "into this mysterious universe we are all plunged at birth with no set of instructions, no maps or signposts"[1]. Some of the tales humans tell themselves come down generation after generation. Others are based on the disciplined and investigatory search for knowledge in this complex world, known as science. Sacred texts, religious and spiritual pronouncements, classical fairy stories, all touch on intuitive truth of a deeper, less obvious kind that is often felt to exist beyond everyday reality. Stories are both moral, and practical. They concern the journey of the person through life, the ordering of society and our relationship with the stars. We are born into a world that is full of mystery, beautiful, violent and

6

often terrifying to human eyes and consciousness. The more we understand the nature of the processes and truths of physical things through modern science, the more awesome the universe becomes. In this amazing structure, we need stories to help make sense of our lives, and to enable societies to function.

The several questions which have fuelled this book are: how much are the political theories we live by at present self-fulfilling prophesies? And how much are they a product of the personal fears, nightmares, deprivations and struggles of their authors? Political philosophies are myths that have hardened into doctrine. They are at least minor and, indeed for some, major myths that societies live out and which deeply influence our own lives and the life of our planet. Can we stand back from the unique way that each creature, including each human being, creates his or her own reality and see more clearly into the roots of the politics, both uniting and divisive, that we have presently created? And could we, with an enlarged and more self-reflexive standpoint, from a different century, develop more comprehensive, less doom-laden stories about the world and the human race than we have now and which could serve us enormously better?

As the anthropologist Ruth Benedict famously wrote, in the language of her time, "No man ever looks at the world with pristine eyes". Even as young babies, we have already started to absorb some of our life-long assumptions, before we are consciously aware and before we can speak or use words. We look and see and are already personally negotiating our place in the surrounding world. And when we begin to use words, there is always a gap between this profound felt experience of life - in so far as we are still in touch with it - and the words we learn to use to share the world with others. We only see what we look at and notice, and we each have a way of seeing which is instinctive. However, the relationship between external knowledge and explanations on the one hand, and the physical, felt and experiential relationship we have with world of which we are a part, including our own being, is never settled, often problematic. But with words, we learn to listen to and tell stories about how things are, to help us live our lives – or, quite often, to put us in our places!

The great myths of every society deal with the great issues: life and death: facing the unknown: the journey of the individual: the nature of men and women: what is right action: relationships with people, society, animals and the natural world: and the invisible but more powerful world that companions our own. As Karen Armstrong writes "mythology was...designed to help us cope with the problematic human predicament. It helped people to find their place in the world and their true orientation"[2]. And myths can often speak to that felt sense in us which is intuitive and deeper than language. They can carry a timelessness beyond the preoccupations of the present, and unite us to a deeper reality.

Joseph Campbell, that determined seeker after deeper truth, speaks as always to the point, when he writes that the stories all humans tell themselves, the living myths of any culture, are firstly and primarily about reconciling human consciousness to the daunting inexorable nature of life and death. For me, he is such an attractive writer and thinker because he looks so widely and deeply, from a framework of the mystery of the cosmos, to the social and community world all living beings inhabit, to the individual awareness of all beings – and back again. He is particularly empowered to do this as he is so knowledgeable about cultures beyond those of the modern West – indigenous and Eastern societies, philosophies and myths specifically.

He emphasises the point that is key to much of the thinking of this book, that in all early societies, and to this day in many Eastern societies, the myths that helped people face death and suffering also contained a great awareness of the sweetness and the value of life, could hold these opposites in their narration, and were world affirming: "through the bitterness of pain, the primary experience at the core of life is a sweet, wonderful thing"[3]. Eastern deities, such as the Hindu gods, demonstrated a mix of opposing qualities – cruelty with love, a numinous presence with mischievous social action, in Kali and Krishna and many other vivid deities.

This contrast of life and death is the issue brought out most vividly and painfully by Darwin from within the western context in the famous last paragraph of *The Origin of Species,* which was modified from one edition to another, depending on the agonising changes of his own views over time about suffering and death:

"It is interesting to contemplate an entangled bank, clothed with many plants of many kinds, with birds singing on the bushes, with various insects flitting about, and with worms crawling through the damp earth, and to reflect that these elaborately constructed forms, so different from one another, and dependent on each other in so complex a manner, have all been produced by the laws acting around us.....Thus, from the war of nature, from famine and from death, the most exalted object which we are capable of conceiving, namely, the production of the higher animals, directly follows. There is grandeur in this view of life, with its several powers, having been originally breathed into a few forms or into one: and that, whilst this planet has gone cycling on according to the fixed law of gravity, from so simple a beginning endless forms most beautiful and most wonderful have been, and are being evolved."[4]

But even in writing this, I can see that Campbell, Darwin and I are all speaking from a particularly Western liberal viewpoint in our expressed concern about universal suffering. From the viewpoint of the majority of humans who have ever lived, usually in far less favourable conditions than our own, over the last hundreds of thousands of years, eating and being eaten has been primary: you killed other animals or people or you died yourself: you avoided predators or you died: your own suffering had to be accepted in that: boys were initiated in many societies into rites designed to enforce courage and make killing a way of living. This is the way things had always been, for ourselves as for other animals.

Myths, world-views, religious scriptures, political theories, social and individual attitudes about the natural world of which we are a part, and self-knowledge, consciousness about ourselves, all involve an attempt to reconcile ourselves with inevitable death, and also almost equally if we are lucky, with the sweetness and beauty of the world we see around us. We need stories at all levels – about the political system we require, about who we are, and about existential questions of living in order to live fruitfully in this situation. And these levels are deeply inter-connected. "What man believes about himself is of the utmost importance", said Edward Sinnott, "for it will determine the kind of world he will make..."[5]. If we try to do politics without self-knowledge or without a wider sense of the earth and the cosmos, then we become (have become we could presently declare) destructive because our politics have no wider context, and are built on sand. If we are only concerned with the individual, then the social and political system is ignored. If we are only bothered about violence and ignore beauty and love, then the wider sense of the universe cannot give us wisdom. We need renewed, wider, deeper, more paradoxical stories than those we presently have.

* * *

Henry Miller, in his play *A Devil in Paradise* makes one of his characters say: "A day like today I realise what I've told you a hundred different times – there is nothing wrong with the world. What's wrong is our way of looking at it".

The wrongness, it seems to me, is not the stories we tell, the rich never-ending supply of myths, philosophies, deep in each culture's history, but it is the conviction, the certainty, of most adherents to their own story, that they are **right**. Myths, world-views, churches, political parties, scientists, tend to see their truth as the only one to follow. But in the nature of things, as soon as you have erected a particular pillar of truth, a solid pointer to the future, you tend to see the positive virtues – and ignore the inevitable shadows thrown by that pillar. Nature is so much more subtle than we are. She values her shadows, her ever-shifting reality, her darkness as much as her light.

Heraclitus, another astute classical Greek thinker, was close to our present chaos and complexity theories, when he indicated that the world was a theatre of perpetual change, of eternal 'Becoming'. The symbol, the archetype, he saw most relevant for the human race, was fire, which was about the continuous change and flow of all things. He saw life as a dance of opposites, much as we find in the Eastern yin/yang diagram, where each easily moves into the other, and the energy produced is life-giving, vital. So, instead of the static formulas we develop today, it could be possible to realise that all factors involved in a social situation, and ourselves with them, are ever changing, always becoming, never fixed. And what will emerge can never be predicted with certainty.

Richard Tarnas, in his brilliant first chapters of *Cosmos and Psyche*, gives us a framework which takes us far into the area of the significance of powerful myths. He contrasts the myth of human 'Progress' through the last 2-3000 years which many in the West hold to, with the equally powerful myth and history of 'The Fall' – the loss of the human relationship with the sacred and the earth, which is seen to result in our present parlous state of constant war and environmental disaster – leading to the extinction of many species which may include much of the human race within the next 100 years or so. Both these stories, of Progress on the one hand and Exile on the other, must have their truth and their limitations. Tarnas writes: "knowledge of history, as of anything else, is ever-shifting, free-floating, ungrounded in an objective reality. Patterns are not so much recognised in phenomena as read into them. History is, finally, only a construct."[6] Indeed, all our myths are only aids to truth, as Xenophanes wrote centuries ago. Wisdom can only come from holding the opposites within any situation we are trying to understand. And you cannot hope to solve many problems on the same level as they occur. Myths are many-layered, some shared, many contradictory.

Furthermore, an increasing number of writers, prompted by a new awareness of the earth and all her creatures, recognise most graphically that humans are not the only species living consciously in this world. Loren Eiseley, a wonderfully poetic naturalist and philosopher, found a teacher in a 'huge yellow-and-black orb spider.' He realises, in his inimitable way, that she too lives an authentic life, when she reacted to his intrusion into her web. He saw that "Spider was circumscribed by spider ideas; its universe was spider universe. All outside was irrational, extraneous, at best, raw material for spider." In fact she was behaving much like the human race. "As I proceeded on my way along the gully, like a vast impossible shadow, I realised that in the world of spider I did not exist.....I began to see that among the many universes in which the world of living creatures existed, some were large, some were small, but that all, including man's, were in some way limited or finite. We were creatures of different dimensions, passing through each others lives like ghosts through doors."[7]. Eiseley felt that we too are webspinners: "let us remember man, the self-fabricator who came across the ice to look into the mirrors and magic of science...he came because he is at heart a listener and a searcher for a transcendental reality beyond himself".

Seeing and understanding more clearly that we live on the earth with many millions of other species, each perceiving 'reality' in its own way, makes us even more aware that reality is about relationship for each living being: a reality mediated by the senses and mindset of the observer with the world around. As I wrote previously in a Quaker pamphlet "All creatures must carry their own world round with them. The elephant, the ant and the bird, though they may at any time be living in a similar space, must be experiencing totally dissimilar worlds, each one feeling like reality. The eye is merely an instrument: the world we see as reality is created in the mind, and the mind of each species and each individual in that species is influenced and informed by experience and learning as well as biology."[8] And as for people, we are particularly influenced by the assumptions and the stories carried within our families, our societies, our education and our explicit or implicit cosmologies about who we are and what we have come to believe in.

These reflections may initially seem some distance away from the political theories with which this book is basically concerned – but, on the contrary, they are most relevant. When I taught political philosophy to first year undergraduates at Brunel University, and what I came to realise over the years, is that political philosophy is in no way a science – it is not tested, researched, proved; it is not a scholarly investigation; it is not a collaborative procedure at all. What each political philosopher does from Machiavelli to Marx and onwards, is to tell a story. Each story starts off with an implicit or explicit view of who we are – what is human nature. Hobbes and Rousseau state their understandings of who we are explicitly, gathered from their own life experience. Then, given their view, they deduce what political system should be created to produce the most favourable society they can envisage. And then, depending on the philosopher's power and influence in society, men in power connect with and become drawn to the truth of the story as they see it and implement the system proposed. Some of the stories – I would say myths – have had immense power in shaping our world. Tom Paine's *Rights of Man* greatly influenced the

American Constitution created in the eighteenth century, as did John Locke's *Two Treatises on Government* and *An essay concerning human understanding*. Karl Marx's *Communist Manifesto* has had enormous power all over the world, and dominated large tracts of the world in Russia, China, South America and parts of Europe. Political myths can and do have enormous power.

The other striking thing that I understood, as I was teaching this material, is that each political theorist is inevitably writing from his own experience of life, telling his own tale. Thomas Hobbes produced his *Leviathan* from a life full of conflict in the English Civil War in the 1640s and from exile; Mary Wollstonecraft wrote her *Vindication of the Rights of Women* in 1794 from a lifetime's experience of being a woman in the eighteenth century. Machiavelli was deeply involved in the wars between the Italian city states in the Renaissance. Also it was interesting to see how many of the writers had experienced very hard child-hoods – though that was almost certainly the norm in the centuries they were writing. But all these factors would have influenced their political sensibilities and perspectives, and the stories they were writing.

These same factors would have affected in particular the views that the writers formed about the nature of human nature, upon which they built their theories. The primary issue in the myths about human nature is not surprisingly identical to that concerning the human cosmological world – and the political one: that issue is the existence of death, cruelty, violence and suffering. In the twentieth century the work of Carl Jung and allied depth psychologists have contributed whole new dimensions to these questions of what have come to be called 'the Shadow'. Sam Keen, an astute American writer comments wryly: "the most terrible of all moral paradoxes, the Gordian Knot that must be unravelled if history is to continue, is that we create evil out of our highest ideals and most noble aspirations. We so need to be heroic, to be on the side of God, to eliminate evil, to clean up the world, to be victorious over death, that we visit destruction and death on all who stand in the way of our heroic historical destiny....In the beginning we create the enemy."[9] This is a very modern psychological take on what is the central question about violence and war as expounded by the classical political philosophers – is the human race intrinsically at war with itself and with the world, which is the strong line taken by Hobbes and Machiavelli: or is the development of civilisation the culprit, as Rousseau suggests – or is the problem the development of capitalism and two opposing classes as proclaimed passionately by Marx? Perhaps humans are capable and even likely to make towards an ever more humane political world with the benefit of education, law and a greater an inclusion of the whole human race in social power as argued by John Stuart Mill? Or are there in the twenty-first century, other issues not yet fully discussed? What do Eastern philosophers such as Gandhi or Confucius, or alternative activists like Winstanley have to add? Pope maintained in the Enlightenment that men are "the glory, jest and riddle of the world" which recognises so succinctly the paradoxes of our nature as manifest in the world. Can we get any further at this point?

In discussing the political philosophers in the first section of the book, I am not intending at all to give any new interpretation of their work. I am however, trying to tease out their basic assumptions, their views of 'who we are', how these assumptions are embedded in their own lives and in the societies in which they live, and the stories they have to tell. I also make some comments on where these ideas have been influential in forming the most powerful political frameworks for society. I am dealing with Britain. There are different slants, different emphases, even in those countries most similar to ourselves: for instance, socialist thought is certainly not mainstream in the USA, and the governments of democratic European countries manifest very different emphases. This First Part of the book traces a dialogue over four centuries and is the political world we have inherited today.

"For all is but a woven web of guesses"

References

1. Young, Louise: *The Unfinished Universe.* Simon and Schuster. 1986. p9
2. Armstrong, Karen: *A Short History of Myth.* Canongate. 2005. p6
3. Campbell, Joseph: *Pathways to Bliss.* New World Library. 2004. p4
4. Darwin, Charles: *The Origin of Species.* Penguin Books 1985. p459
5. Young, Louise op.cit. p185
6. Tarnas, Richard: *Cosmos and Psyche.* Viking. 2006. p15.
7. Eiseley, Loren: *The Unexpected Universe.* Harvest/HBJ book. 1969. pp50/51
8. Hardy, Jean: *There is another world but it is this one.* Quaker Universalist Group. UK. 1995
9. Keen, Sam: *The Enemy Maker,* pp197-202: in Zwieg Connie and Abrams Jeremiah: *Meeting the Shadow: the hidden part of the Dark Side of Human Nature.* Jeremy Tarcher. 1991

Part One

Chapter Two

Machiavelli, Hobbes and Burke. The early search for order to control unruly humanity.

And new philosophy calls all in doubt,
The element of fire is quite put out;
The sun is lost, and th'earth, and no man's wit
Can well direct him where to look for it.
And freely men confess that this world's spent,
When in the planets, and the firmament
They seek so many new; they see that this
Is crumbled out again to his atomies.
'Tis all in pieces, all coherence gone;
All just supply, and all relation.......
This is the world's condition now....

John Donne,1612
An Anatomy of the World pp 205-19.

Here we are at the beginning of the modern period, with the stories which have created our present world. I start with the great poet John Donne, who was commenting on the tremendous changes which were then reaching England from the Continent. New beliefs were powerfully destroying the old medieval world with its relative certainty and its intrinsic coherence of religious belief, social structure and understanding of the place of the human in the universe: and creating a new world of revolution, the overturning of structures and knowledge, beginning with the Renaissance, the Reformation of religion, the 'new philosophy' and radical science and cosmology. The English monarchy itself was threatened and the 'Divine Right' of kings to rule questioned. The forces behind these movements led to the English Civil War of the 1640s and eventually the beheading of King Charles 1 in 1649.

Our two first philosophers lived respectively at the beginning and the end of this early modern period. Niccolo Machiavelli, usually accounted the first modern political philosopher, lived in Italy 100 years before Donne's poem, from 1469-1527, at the beginning of the Italian Renaissance. He published his major book *The Prince* in 1513: this is advice to Princes ruling the city states on how to gain and maintain power. He is usually seen as the first modern Western political philosopher. He was a citizen of Florence at a time of constant war between the city states, was a diplomat and writer, and suffered a considerable period in prison.

Thomas Hobbes' *Leviathan* was published 140 years after *The Prince,* in 1651, and was based on his experience of conflict and exile related to the violence and bitterness of the English Civil War. War and strife were fundamental to the lives of both Machiavelli and Hobbes, and their political books and their lives were an attempt to make sense of their experience at this time. For both, Donne's phrase "'Tis all in pieces, all coherence gone" was fundamentally the truth. All three men were, as we are today, trying to break through to new reality, a new framework, a new story, which would make sense of a changing world.

In the middle ages, where the political and social system was embedded in a rigid hierarchical network of mutual obligation, authority and power were seen to reflect the natural and sacred order of the universe, and the law seen as "eternal, universal, absolute"[1]. Joseph Campbell emphasises this coherence even more significantly when he writes; "in the total view of the medieval thinkers there was a perfect accord between the structure of the universe, the canons of the social order, and the good of the individual".[2] But, as Hanna Pitkin writes in her feisty book on Machiavelli, "for the medieval sense that dependence is natural and that 'someone else is in charge', the Renaissance substituted a lively consciousness of human self-creation – both the individual shaping his character and career, and the community shaping itself through history......authority was becoming internalised" (see endnotes). This is the voice of the modern mode.

Machiavelli's book *The Prince* looked for inspiration to the classic Roman writers for his advice on politics and power: the classic Greek and Roman writers were the major source of wisdom for all the writers and artists of the Renaissance. His book is basically advice to Princes – that is, leaders holding power of a state – on how to gain and handle power, and how to hold on to effective leadership.

Machiavelli had been involved for some years in international negotiation as an ambassador in Europe, particularly Italy, for Florence. However, just before 1511 the Medici family regained power in Florence. He was subsequently imprisoned and tortured, accused of complicity against the Medici, and on his release fled from Florence. Having been both an ambassador and a prisoner (not an unusual combination in those turbulent times), he reckoned he had something of wisdom to say.

His book is about a leader's need for powerful manhood, and on the ubiquity and necessity of war. He taught that the desire for war is deep and permanent in men - specifically men. In *The Discourses* he writes: "Whenever there is no need for men to fight, they fight for ambition's sake: and so powerful is the sway that ambition exercises over the human heart that they never relinquish it, no matter how high they have risen. The reason is that nature has so constituted men that, though all things are objects of desire, not all things are attainable, with the result that men are ill content with what they possess and their present state brings them little satisfaction". In other words, he sees the human situation as one of discontent. Men naturally fight: they want glory and possessions. "Dependence is characteristic of women, children and animals; for men it is despicable and fatally dangerous"[3]

Because war is so important, central to society in his view, then whether you are at war or at 'peace' – in other words, not actually fighting – then everything in society ought to be geared towards winning – the economy, business, government should all be conducted with war in mind. The successful Prince is the one who adapts himself to the times. What came to the fore in Italy in the Renaissance was the idea, foreign to the medieval period where custom ruled, and indeed to most periods before, that a political order can be set up deliberately. You can think out how to run a state from scratch, depending on the view you have of people and society. Politics in the Renaissance comes to be seen as different from morals, and from religion.

In such a society, it is acceptable, indeed necessary, for those in power to wear a mask. It is dangerous to show your real self – and that mask may come to be so habitual, that you might in fact lose sight of who you are as a private person. Human nature is despicable in general and therefore order is of paramount importance as an external curb, to control the worst excesses of which we are capable. But you *can* develop a good state if the Prince has enough self-knowledge and knowledge of others and of the times, where people can come to see that it is in their own interests to contribute to the common good. All men want order; only a few want freedom and know what it is.

What people fear most is the vagaries of fortune – in fact Machiavelli would come to call her Fortune, the myth expressing the power of this often hostile world. Chapter 25 in *The Prince* is very lyrical and specific on this point: "I hold it to be true that Fortune is the arbiter of one-half of our actions, but that she still leaves us to direct the other half, or perhaps a little less. I compare her to one of those raging rivers, which when in flood overflows the plains, sweeping away trees and buildings, bearing away the soil from place to place; everything flies before it, all yield to its violence, without being able in any way to withstand it; and yet, though its nature be such, it does not follow therefore that men, when the weather becomes fair, shall not make provision, both with defences and barriers, in such a manner that, rising again, the waters may pass away by canal, and their force be neither so unrestrained nor so dangerous." In other words, if the leader and his followers can be cunning and ingenious, like the fox which is one of Machiavelli's favourite images, we can learn to guard much of the worst that the world can throw at us as a society.

At the end of Chapter 25, Machiavelli makes one of his most infamous statements: "For my part, I consider that it better to be adventurous than cautious, because fortune is a woman, and if you wish to keep her under it is necessary to beat and ill-use her; and it is seen that she allows herself to be mastered by the adventurous rather than those who go to work more coldly. She is therefore, always, woman-like, a lover of young men, because they are less cautious, more violent, and with more audacity command her." It would be difficult to find a more misogynous statement!

Machiavelli considered that the worst thing is to be dependent, effeminate, powerless. According to Hanna Pitkin's interesting book, "the feminine constitutes 'the other' for Machiavelli, opposed to manhood and autonomy in all their senses: to maleness, to adulthood, to humanness, and to politics."[4] Without doing anything, women motivate men to cause political trouble, and have been very destructive of order.

It is interesting to see written into political discourse, right from the beginning of the modern period, specific and explicit material about the rejection of 'the other'. In Machiavelli's material, the Other is the female and natural forces, the earth, against which men and ordered social forces have to hold out and exert control. He also considers the area of self knowledge, believing it to be desirable, indeed necessary in the leader of a successful state. But this awareness may need to be masked for your own protection. And it may mean that a 'vice' in the right place will bring you more security and prosperity than a virtue in the wrong one.

* * *

One hundred and forty years later, in England, in 1651, Thomas Hobbes published his book *Leviathan*. A Leviathan is a sea monster, of enormous size, and it was to a leviathan that Hobbes was likening the absolute Monarch or the modern State: "The Matter, Forme and Power of a Common-Wealth, Ecclesiasticall and Civill" is the sub-title of the book. The State, he writes, is a huge human structure. He specifies that the book is "occasioned by the disorders of the present time." And these were disorders indeed. A bitter civil war was fought in England between 1642 and 1648 between the Cavaliers – the King, Charles I, his supporters, and the Catholic church on the one hand and the Roundheads, Parliament, Protestants, much of the army, Oliver Cromwell, and radical thinkers on the other. For much of that period, there was no censorship on writers and many radical pamphlets were published. The Roundheads won and in January 1649, the unthinkable - many thought blasphemous- happened, the King was executed. Until then, English monarchs had ruled by divine right and were believed to be the true representatives of God on the earth.

In publishing *Leviathan* two years later, Hobbes was responding to a great need – a need for a legitimated workable way of governing the country and a whole new system of thinking about human society. Thomas Hobbes was a graduate of Oxford, who searched his classical education in Greek and Latin for some insights into men and government. He worked with Francis Bacon and was drawn into the new science, particularly its search for knowledge through reasoning, deduction from proof and experiment. He travelled in Europe, met Galileo and became fascinated by the ideas of motion and change, developing new truths by working on a hypothesis. In the 1630s he planned a systematic philosophy, or science, of Body, the nature of Man, and the Citizen. In 1640 he produced *Elements of Law, Natural and Politic.* Shortly afterwards he fled to Paris because of the growing hostilities in England and stayed there in exile until 1650.

"Hobbes is widely, and rightly, regarded as the most formidable of English political theorists; formidable, not because he is difficult to understand but because his doctrine is at once so clear, so sweeping, and so disliked. His postulates about the nature of man are unflattering, his political conclusions are illiberal, and his logic appears to deny us any way out."[5]

Thomas Hobbes famously envisages a 'state of nature' in which men lived before ordered society, deducing this from his observation of their behaviour in ordinary society, and concluding that their basic behaviour 'is either for gain or glory; that is, not so much for love of our fellows, as for love of themselves'[6]

In *Leviathan* he puts forward his famous doctrines some of which are worth expounding in full as they are so clear. He depicts man and state as microcosm and macrocosm in society: they share the same characteristics. Because men are constantly searching for power, and are more or less equal in physical strength, the natural condition of mankind is war. This he knows partly through self-knowledge and partly through observation. In Chapter 11 he writes "so, in the first place, I put for a general inclination of all mankind, a perpetual and restless desire of power after power, that ceaseth only in Death. And the cause of this, is not always that a man hopes for a more intense delight, than he has already attained to: or that he cannot be content with a more moderate Power: but because he cannot assure the power and means to live well, which he hath present, without the acquisition of more." Men love themselves best, have insatiable desires and want more and more are never satisfied.

This is a search for more and more wealth, goods, power, which is never-ending. It is described by Macpherson, in a well-known book, as possessive individualism, a condition under which we all live in our rationalist, acquisitive and competitive societies, now spread round the world, to this day.

Because of this constant competition, modern societies need strong laws, strong controls in society, and strong family structures that can control their children against the child's worst impulses, so that order can prevail. If order is not maintained in this authoritarian way at all levels of society, then the society itself comes to be in a virtual state of war. When men live without any social security, then they have to depend on their own inadequate strength – but then "in such condition, there is no place for Industry; because the fruit thereof is uncertain: and consequently no Culture of the Earth; no navigation, nor use of the commodities that may be imported by Sea; no commodious building….no Knowledge of the face of the Earth; no account of Time; no Arts; no Letters; no Society; and which is worst of all, continuall feare, and danger of violent death; And the life of man, solitary, poore, nasty, brutish and short"[7].

However, if the right mechanisms of control are put into place into society at every level, from the family to the state, then people will be induced to live in peace and order. Their behaviour will be modified to fit in and society will work like a competent machine. One of the most powerful mechanisms of control is economic. Market relationships are seen as the basis of all other working relationship, including marriage. The Commonwealth, or State, is a human construct. "The skill of making, and maintaining Commonwealths, consists in certain rules, as doth arithmetic and geometry; not (as tennis play) upon practice only; which Rules, neither poor men have the leisure, nor men that have the leisure, have hitherto had the curiosity, or the method, to find out"[8]. Many animals, like ants and bees, live sociably naturally, and don't have the manipulative curiosity of human beings! But people need an explicit understanding and system about society in order to devise a method that works. That is what *Leviathan* was trying to do – and did do, to great effect – to develop a way of thinking which is powerful to this day.

One of the natural curbs on men is wages. "The value or Worth of a man, is as of all other things, his Price; that is to say, so much as would be given for the use of his Power: and therefore is not absolute.....For let a man (as most men do) rate themselves as the highest value they can; yet their true value is no more than it is esteemed by others" (Chapter 10). As Macpherson writes: "Market society brought with it an objective order which did not require any transcendental moral forces to keep it functioning"[9]. That too, supported by many subsequent writers, notably Adam Smith, created a Western mode of living which is still immensely powerful in the societies in which we live today.

* * *

Edmund Burke lived a hundred years on from Thomas Hobbes within the eighteenth century – 1729-1797 are his dates. I feel he comes in the same category as Machiavelli and Hobbes because he held that evil is inherent in human nature, and that Government exists to restrain the imperfections springing from this negative characteristic. He reckoned that order is funda-mental to a viable society, and this has to be maintained despite our less desirable, and indeed evil, qualities. He is usually seen to be the first fully fledged Conservative in the British system.

Burke's views were modified however by several other factors. He was for religious diversity though assumed all should hold a religious belief: he wrote "we know, and it is our pride to know, that man is by constitution a religious animal: that atheism is against not only our reason but against our instincts". He distrusted reason when it was cut off from feeling and theory unless it was based on practice. Both Machiavelli and Hobbes would have agreed with the latter, though not necessarily with the former.

He had a strong deep view of the nature of society itself. He reckoned that any old society was very complex and contained its own longstanding wisdom. It contained an ancient and continuing social order. He wrote that the social contract is "a partnership not only between those who are living, but between those who are living, those who are dead, and those who are to be born."[10]. He valued societies that had a strong sense of their own traditions, beliefs and mystery and celebrated them, as against the narrowing uniformity and egalitarianism and utilitarianism of the most radical systems.

His religious and social views came together in supporting the class system as given. "The awful author of our being is the author of our place in the order of existence; and that having disposed and marshalled us by a divine tactic, not according to our will, but according to his, he has....virtually subjected us to act the part which belongs to the place assigned to us."[11] He had little time for the state of nature, and thought that civilisation was a welcome change from the anarchy he supposed it superseded. He stated his strong position: to keep an established church, an established monarchy, an established aristocracy and an established (limited) democracy. He also thought that politics themselves were pretty marginal to society under those conditions, and should not be taken too seriously or treated with reverence: the government should consistent of as few as possible virtuous and wise men.

Once the contract of a society is agreed, which may be through time or ratified at a particular juncture, there is no reason to alter it: nor any reason to alter the distribution of land or goods. He had little sympathy and nothing to give to the poor.

He believed there should be "equal rights but not to equal things."

Burke believed that respect for authority is natural. The family, the 'little platoon' in society, together with inherited property, is the foundation of the nation

Edmund Burke's views take on a myth-like quality when he writes of the power of society. "The individual is foolish; the multitude, for the moment, are foolish, when they act without deliberation; but the species is wise, and, when time is given to it, as a species it always acts right...The state of civil society ....is a state of nature; and much more truly so than a savage or incoherent mode of life. For man is by nature reasonable; and he is never perfect in his natural state, but when he is placed where reason may be best cultivated and best predominates"[12]. Then he can fulfil his greatest potential, and so therefore can society. Liberty can therefore be best associated with good government and social order.

Burke's key book *Reflections on the Revolution in France* came out a year after the French Revolution, not surprisingly, and was a deep and impassioned protest against that revolutionary coup against the Monarchy, religion and property rights. He said the leaders "loved mankind but hated man".

In his writings he created a conservative myth of society and politics, where society was predominant and held quite mystical power, and where formal politics was reduced to the background.

* * *

These three men were part of the foundation of political philosophy which has come to be known as conservatism. To this day, the doctrines and myths developed above, are proclaimed by conservative politicians. Chris Patten in '*The Tory Case*' published in 1983 spells modern assumptions spells out fully and explicitly:

"Man was created in the image of God but he is flawed; he inherits Adam's mistake. He is capable therefore of great evil as well as great good. Hitler and St Francis of Assisi are both members of the human race.......Without authority, government and the law, the impulses of an imperfect man are as like to lead him to do what is wrong as to do what is right"[13].

There is always a fear in traditional Conservative thinking that things could get worse: that order is kept against a constant fear of chaos – or in Machiavelli's case, uncontrollable Fortune. It emphasises the significance of tradition, of a strong family in which parents can control and hopefully eradicate the more undesirable traits of their children. There is no doubt that life is a fight of good against evil, and that the side you are on is good. Machiavelli of course has his own particular take on this, not living in a bourgeois society: for him it was fear - of Fortune, of the female and the 'effeminate', of enemies - that made him need the strength of an authoritarian regime. But all conservatives look for the permanency of institutions, and a strong sense of your own rightness against the enemy.

Lord Salisbury well represents conservative belief in the nineteenth century. He is deeply pessimistic about human nature and doubtful about the idea of progress. He comments: "how thin is the crust which the habits of civilisation, however ancient and unbroken, draw over the boiling lava of human passion. Whenever the Anglo Saxon race has been free for a few years from any movements of open violence, there have always been certain philosophers eager to catch at the belief that the need of curbing human nature has gone by and that the millennium of 'enlightened selfishness is dawning' "[14].

The class system is seen as right and proper, and properly backed up by the Church. The upper classes have the right to lead. But they should be fair in their wisdom. And if tradition, patriotism and order do the job of maintaining a peaceful social system, then there is no need for a heavy political presence or any blueprints for the future. Unruly humanity can be ruled at last.

References

1. Pitkin, Hanna Fenchel: *Fortune is a Woman: Gender and Politics in the thought of Nicola Machiavelli.* University of California Press. 1984 p9.
2. Campbell, Joseph: *Myths to live by.* Condor 1972.
3. Pitkin op.cit. p11
4. Pitkin op cit. p22
5. Pitkin op.cit. p109
6. Macpherson,C.B.: *The Political Theory of Possessive Individualism.* Oxford University Press. 1962. p9
7. Macpherson op.cit. p27
8. Hobbes, Thomas: *Leviathan.* Penguin 1984. Chapter 13.
9. Hobbes op cit. Chapter 20
10. Macpherson. Introduction to *Leviathan.* p58
11. O'Gorman, Frank: *Edmund Burke: His political philosophy.* 2004. p.15, from *Reflections from the Revolution in France. 1790*
12. Edmund Burke: *Appeal from the New to the Old Whigs 1791: Reflections on the Revolution in France*
13. Chris Patten: *The Tory Case.* Longman 1983. p25
14. Pinto-Duschinsky, Michael: *The Political Thought of Lord Salisbury.* p91

Chapter Three

John Locke, J.S. Mill and F.A.Hayek
The rise of individualism, capitalism and the rational man.

What a piece of worke is a man! How Noble in Reason!
how infinite in faculties! In form and moving how
express and admirable! In action how like an Angel!
In apprehension how like a God! the beauty of the
World! The paragon of animals! And yet, to me,
what is this Quintessence of Dust? Man delights not
me; no, nor woman either, though by your smiling
you seem to say so.

William Shakespeare, Hamlet. Act 2 Scene 2 285-300

Shakespeare was a man of the Renaissance, born in 1564, dying
in 1616. And how here he expresses the Renaissance spirit –
glorying in the individual man – and yet at the same time deeply
suspicious. The words are both quintessential – as he uses the
word -and intimate. That we regard ourselves as 'individuals' is
perhaps the most significant characteristic of the modern
Western era. We take it for granted that we have our own distinct
personality, our own beliefs and attitudes. The whole education
system, particularly as it has applied to all children in the last
two hundred years, fosters this sense of uniqueness and
separateness. We tend to feel ourselves subjects as against the
objectivity of the rest of the world. We now probably, formed by
our culture and education have developed a sense of individuality exceptional in the history of the planet.

Many, perhaps most, humans assume that individuality

applies only to humans. This important assumption will be discussed later in the book, but in general in our society it is this general view that has counted. Locke, Mill and Hayek would doubtless agree with the human centred concept. It was a notion of the importance of the individual human being, the significance of the miraculousness and wonder of mankind that the Renaissance first emphasised, his dignity and blessedness in the universe. It is well known that in this period artists started painting people as different from one another, with particular idiosyncratic characteristics: the human face comes to be of particular interest. Elizabethan drama in England emphasises the interplay between subtly and vividly drawn personalities, especially of course in Shakespeare. The awareness of individuality in humans changed social, political, religious and economic life in the changeover from the medieval to the modern period, especially as the Protestant, particularly the puritan, influence advanced through Europe.

In the seventeenth and eighteenth centuries, not only was the notion of 'the person' changing, but with it the basis of the economic system. Until the beginnings of the seventeenth century usury – lending money for interest – was regarded not only as a sin in Christianity, but also as a crime. You could be executed for committing it. This changed with the growth of the market system, the massive increase in national and international trading, and competition at every level. Usury in Britain had been de-criminalised in an Act in 1545 *The restraint of Usury* where permission was given to charge interest on lent money: by 1620, Ruston defines that "usury had passed from being an offence against public morality which a Christian government was expected to suppress to being a matter of private conscience (and) a new generation of Christian moralists redefined usury as excessive interest".[1]

Land as well as money was seen as capital, and increasingly a man's labour was perceived as a capital asset he (as it usually was) could sell, which was also subject to the law of the market. The biggest political preoccupation by the end of the seventeenth century was the law of property in all its manifestations: and also the way this related to the changing political system, which from the return of Charles II in 1660, was that of a beginning Parliamentary democracy headed by the Monarchy, made law by the English Revolution of 1688.

Locke's *Two Treatises of Government* was published two years afterwards in 1690; it is the second Treatise which is key to the principles he set out. The Principles he advocated, building on the clear model set by Hobbes, are so important that they have become almost a myth in themselves – the story of a representative democracy in which government is by consent and with the goodwill of the governed. It is also based upon the theory of what Macpherson calls 'possessive individualism' as its economic basis. He defines this as having seven main propositions which include:

i) what makes a man human is freedom from dependence on the will of others, except those agreements he enters into voluntarily in his own interests

ii) the individual is essentially the proprietor of his own person and capacities, for which he owes nothing to society

iii) political society is a human contrivance for the protection of the individual's property in his person and in his goods, and therefore for the maintenance of orderly relations of exchange between individuals as proprietors of themselves and

iv) human society is essentially a series of market relations.

John Locke, perhaps the most influential political theorist in the history of Britain, and indeed in the early part of the newly developing U.S.A., was born in 1632 and died in 1704: he was at

Westminster School at the time of the execution at Westminster of Charles I. His father had fought in the Parliamentary army. After taking a degree at Oxford, he trained as a doctor, but also worked for the Earl of Shaftesbury, who became Lord Chancellor. He then led a full life in medicine and politics. For a variety of reasons he eventually withdrew from an active involvement of national politics, and lived the last fourteen years of his life in retirement. He met and was influenced both by Rene Descartes and Isaac Newton.

It is instructive to read some of the actual vivid words he used in the Second Treatise. He said in Chapter 5.27: "Though the earth and all inferior creatures be common to all men, yet every man has a 'property' in his own 'person'. This nobody has any right to but himself. The 'labour' of his body and the 'work' of his hands, we may say, are properly his. Whatsoever, then, he removes out of the state that Nature has provided and left it in, he has mixed his labour with it, and joined it to something that is his own, and thereby makes it his property". This is essentially how you acquire land and any made goods in a rural society. Could there be a more significant statement for our present world? Its incorporation into government, law and politics led to the industrial revolution, to a global economy, and by assuming the earth and her creatures are something we can use for our convenience, to the present trashing and exploitation of the earth: to climate change and the extinction of many species: and to the enormous wealth mankind has created, using the earth as his resource. This was also, in Locke's words, sanctioned by the Christian God, in the expectation that mankind will use his common sense, his reason, in how to go about it: "God , who hath given the world to men in common, hath also given them reason to make use of it to the best advantage of life and convenience". God, he saw as the great Property Owner, and that basically we are all responsible to God for the way we live here. But what was hardly taken into account in this conception was that the earth herself is the sole originator of all the resources, wealth and opportunity.

Locke, more than Hobbes, saw something of the downside of his propositions. He acknowledged that men had possessions in different proportions – some became rich, others poor, which is a matter of concern. He like most people at that time assumed that it was only the educated, the bourgeoisie, as we have come to call them, who could understand the matters he was writing about. In a later publication of 1695 *The Reasonableness of Christianity* he wrote: "the greatest part of mankind have not the labour for learning and logick, and superfine distinction of the schools. Where the hand is used to the plough and the spade, the head is seldom elevated to fine notions, or exercised in mysterious reasoning. Tis well if men of that rank (to say nothing of the other sex) can comprehend plain propositions, and a short reasoning about things familiar to their minds, and nearly applied to their experience. Go beyond this, and you amaze the greatest part of mankind….." For "the day–labourers and the traders, the spinsters and the dairy-maids….hearing plain commands, is the sure and only course to bring them to obedience and practice. The greatest part cannot know, and therefore they must believe." In this most revealing statement to be considered later, as in his propositions, he was missing out the majority of men and all of women as he assumed they could not understand what he was talking about. John Locke added that we are all 'white paper, void of all characters when we are born', and education is vital to true understanding of the nature of human life. Again it would only be the free men who would receive that education and would be capable of benefiting from it. However, as can be seen from this statement, Locke did not assume that men were born evil: on the contrary, he thought they were born blank.

In a highly unequal social system, the rich, in amassing money as capital, were given the wherewithal to build industries and cities, which he regarded as a benefit. R.H.Tawney, in his classic review of the start of this whole dynamic, *Religion and the Rise of Capitalism*, maintained that the world came to be seen as existing not to be enjoyed but to be conquered in the new capitalist era.

By the nineteenth century, these aspects of modern life, this new individualism and capitalism, in society, economics and politics, had come to define the modern era especially for the middle classes. This was a period when the liberal consciousness could flourish, and the individual be seen to come into full flower as a social being. John Stuart Mill expressed for the nineteenth century what came to be seen as the liberal political view in his books *On Liberty* 1861, *Representative Government* 1869 and *Subjection of Women* 1869. He lived from 1806 to 1873.

Mill had a strong sense of the particularity of each individual within the social and political system. Each person may have a 'plan of life' which will be unique, and his happiness depends on the possibilities life offers to fulfil that plan. His basic value is freedom, though he reckoned this was only fully realised when a person was mature (and educated) enough to be able to pursue it. This meant inevitably there would be a two-tiered society where some will have attained maturity and others need to be led. "Human nature is not a machine to be built after a model, and set to do exactly the work prescribed for it, but a tree, which requires to grow and develop itself on all sides, according to the tendency of inward forces which make it a living thing".[2] This however could only be fully realised if you had the education and subsequent opportunity to realise your potential.

Benign change in society can be brought about by the interaction of these mature and unique people, together with the scientific investigation of the material world which had become possible in the nineteenth century in the West. We are formed by the culture of society but with insight can guide ourselves in the most self-fulfilling paths; we can negotiate with others to subdue the most destructive elements in ourselves, and work politically towards common goals.

However, he thought that society in general was not mature enough to operate a direct, or participatory government, so that the very limited representative system is the most appropriate at the present time. The important factor in governing modern societies is that individuals are left alone as much as possible by the state. His famous phrase was that everyone should be free to do as he likes "so long as he doesn't injure his neighbour", but of course that is the crux of the problems of society today. We constantly risk injuring our neighbours, human and other species, through our actions especially if we are rich and relatively powerful.

Mill believed that a major problem in modern society is the roles that people, men and women alike, are called upon to play. Adherence to the social system leads to a terrible conformity, politically and socially, and is a barrier to truly realising ourselves. Liberals believe that human nature is intrinsically the same, in intelligence, in emotional disposition, and does not vary with sex, class, race or religion. Mill, greatly influenced by his wife, Harriet Taylor, felt particularly strongly about the 'subjection of women'. "The ideas and institutions by which the accident of sex is made the groundwork of an inequality of legal rights, and a forced dissimilarity of social functions, must ere long be recognised as the greatest hindrance to moral, social and even intellectual improvement".[3] Women at that period had few political or social rights. Their property became their husband's at marriage. They had few rights in relation to their children, and were subject to their husbands sexually and legally. Formal education wasn't open to women, at school or university level. Their duties were seen entirely in relation to their husbands or fathers, and it was assumed that the family was where they would find their greatest satisfaction. Mill commented that women's nature is like a tree that has been reared half in a vapour-bath and half in the snow – "forced repression in some directions, unnatural stimulation in others". But this was entirely due to social pressures and norms, and nothing to do with women's intrinsic nature.

Freidrich A.Hayek in the twentieth century wrote a biography of J.S.Mill and Harriet Taylor. Hayek was born in Austria in 1899 and died in 1992. He moved to the London School of Economics in 1931, and after 20 years went to the University of Chicago as Professor of Social and Moral Philosophy, moving back to Freiberg in Germany in 1967. He wrote his main political, very controversial, book *The Road to Serfdom* in the middle of the Second World War In it he speaks for individualism and against any form of socialism. If liberalism can be extreme, this is it.

"During the whole of this modern period of European history the general direction of social development was one of freeing the individual from the ties which had bound him to the customary or prescribed ways.......wherever the barriers to the free exercise of human ingenuity were removed man became rapidly able to satisfy ever-widening ranges of desire."[4] This freedom had meant the burgeoning expansion of science and technology, financial freedom and wealth production. This vast improvement in living standards benefited poor people as well as rich, so that they achieved a degree of material comfort, security and personal independence which was unprecedented in human history. The function of government he saw as being like a good gardener – ready to nurture the plants, take out the weeds, but basically to let the natural forces of society flourish without too much interference. He was close to Margaret Thatcher's view that there is no such thing as society, only individuals. But he believed that liberalism had reached its zenith by the end of the nineteenth century. In England, even more strikingly in Germany, state planning and control, socialism in all its forms where government was intervening and engineering society to achieve its ends, had started to predominate. He quotes de Tocqueville who wrote in 1848:

"Democracy extends the sphere of individual freedom, socialism restricts it. Democracy attaches all possible value to each man; socialism makes each man a mere agent, a mere number. Democracy and socialism have nothing in common but one word: equality. But notice the difference: while democracy seeks equality in liberty, socialism seeks equality in restraint and servitude."[5]

His strong argument was that he saw that the Russian Revolution of 1917, which was called Marxist or Socialist, and the rise of Hitler in Germany in 1933, which was called National Socialist or Fascist, as all one phenomenon. Though the two regimes looked like the opposite ends of the political extremes – Far Left or Far Right, he thought they were fundamentally the same: totalitarian; violent; repressive of individual freedom. He argued that democratic socialism, which had been the strong hope of reformers, had been the "great utopia of the last few generations", was both unachievable and highly dangerous. It is, he argues, the element of central planning and organisation that is the most dangerous element: bureaucratisation the enemy. The attempt at security is chosen at the cost of true freedom.

Hayek also of course believed in a free market, left to the natural forces of the market. He wanted at all levels an impersonal system that ran itself, in economics and in society at large. His liberal view was supported strongly by Maynard Keynes, who said *The Road to Serfdom* was a "grand book". It is certainly the liberal view brought effectively into the violent twentieth century.

References

1. Ruston R. *Does it matter what we do with our money?* Priests and People 1993. in Visser W.A.M. & McIntosh Alistair article on Usury in Accounting, Business & Financial History. www.Lariba Journal 1998 pp175-189
2. Mill J.S.: *On Liberty*

3.   Mill J.S.: *Principles of Political Economy*
4.   Hayek F.A.:*The Road to Serfdom*.Routledge & Kegan Paul 1944 pp11/12
5.   op cit. de Tocqueville. Collected Works vol 1X p546 1866.

Chapter Four

The Search for Economic Equality

Methought I saw how wealthy men
Did grind the poor men's faces
And greedily did prey on them,
Not pitying their cases;
They make them toil and labour sore
For wages too, too small;
The rich men in the tavern roar,
But poor men pay for all.

Methought I saw a usurer old
Walk in his fox-furred gown,
Whose wealth and eminence controlled
The most men in the town;
His wealth he by extortion got,
And rose by others' fall;
He had what his hands earned not,
And poor men pay for all.

Current in 1640s England

The search for greater equality, eventually known as socialism
cannot be presented just by its writers. There are too many of
them. And socialism has always been demonstrated by action,
not just words and philosophy. The urge towards equality and
freedom for all in England is generally reckoned to have begun
in the fourteenth century. It was in 1381 that Wat Tyler in the first
great popular uprising against both religious and state taxes,
asserted "that all men should be free, and of one condition". This

conviction sprang not only from a growing protest against the medieval power structure, which exerted complete economic and personal domination over the mass of people, but also from the teachings of Jesus Christ whose teachings became more available because of the growing use of English in Churches. As John Ball said in the following century at the revolts in 1414, "we are all sons of Adam, born free".

But it is in the 17th century that the radical nature of the protest became effective – so effective that for eleven years, the power of the monarchy was toppled in the apocalyptic and previously unthinkable act, the execution of the King, King Charles I. The Civil War in England 1642-8 was of course more than a revolt about economic equality. It was for the protesters, a fundamental uprising against the status quo: a search for a transformed society: a 'world turned upsidedown'. For the most radical movements, the Levellers, the Diggers, the Seekers and Shakers, this was a revolt against the laws of property and land; as Winstanley asked, urging universal equality: "was the earth made for to preserve a few covetous, proud men, to live at ease, and for them to bag and barn up the treasures of the earth from others, that they might beg and starve in a fruitful land, or was it made to preserve all her children? Let Reason, and the Prophets' and Apostles' writings be judge, the earth is the Lord's, it is not to be confined to particular interest."[1] Just after this, Winstanley, the leader of the Diggers, took possession of common land on St George's Hill, Walton-on-Thames, with members of the Diggers community where they lived for some eighteen months. It was his belief that humans by becoming free could become fulfilled within themselves and become truly wise. "Hell exists in man because of the evil organisation of society, and the conception is then used to perpetuate that society by those who benefit from it."[2] As Colonel Rainborough, one of leaders in the New Model Army declared in the famous Putney Debates of 1647, "the poorest he that is in England hath a life to live as the greatest he", and he asked in regard to wealth and property, "how it comes about that there is such a property in some freeborn Englishmen and not in others" under what he regarded as the tyrannous system of natural and common law.[3] Indeed, it seems to me that that the search for equality, wisdom and community in the 1640s was closer to the new genuine politics many of us might still seek for today than any other.

Winstanley thought that wisdom is inborn, that all people should have a regard to their own experience and inner feeling, and believe less what other people tell them. He wanted formal education for all, but also that people should learn manual dexterity, learning how to do and make things, along with book learning. Private property and inequality he thought corrupting for all concerned: evil is what we learn by living in a damaged and damaging society, not what we are born with. He believed that Christ was a symbol of human potential, what we could all be if society were better. He was nearer than any other thinker to seeing religious and political truth as being myths, truths expressed symbolically.

That extraordinary period of the 1640s has left such a rich literature in pamphlets written by truly radical thinkers and activists because for almost eight years of the Civil War there was no censorship. The proposals were politically radical and many deeply spiritual: this was the period when the Quaker movement began. It was a time when old certainties were dying, new and deeply imaginative visions were arising. Would we could, and will, produce such a rich emergence of value-laden possibilities for a different world today.

Modern socialism did not appear however until two hundred years later. French philosophers coined the word 'socialism' in 1832, after the French Revolution, to refer to the movements fighting against injustices in industrial capitalism. The British word 'socialism' is dated about 1839, with the writings and actions of Robert Owen, and the rise of the Chartist and eventually Trade Union movements.

Robert Owen published his *New View of Society* in 1831. Like most political philosophers, he started with explicit premises about human nature. His view, from his position as a man of property, wealth and power, was that "man's character is made for, not by, him" and that education and environment should enable our better nature to develop. He thought that government and the nature of any given society formed the citizens within. Like Locke, but unlike Winstanley, he believed that human nature is plastic and infinitely malleable.[4] "It must be evident to those who have been in the practice of observing children with attention, that much of good and evil is taught or acquired by a child at a very early period of its life; that much of temper and or disposition is correctly or incorrectly formed before he attains his second year; and that many durable impressions are made at the termination of the first twelve or even six months of his existence". Shades, a century before, of Freud and Winnicott! However, unlike them he believed more strongly in determinism, that a person cannot form his own character.

Robert Owen was in the position, because of his wealth and standing, as a factory owner, of being able to provide the environment for families which he believed to be of most benefit to them. He set up at New Lanark the factory and school, a whole community where optimum conditions could prevail. "On the experience of life devoted to the subject, I hesitate not to say, that the members of a community may by degrees learn to live without violence, without poverty, without crime, and without punishment: for each of these is the effect of error in the various systems prevalent throughout the world. They are all necessary consequences of ignorance." He was working towards a National Plan of Character (he would have probably looked with some approval of many of the manifestations of our present 'nanny state'). He, like Sidney and Beatrice Webb after him, believed strongly in rationality: he was one of the first modern writers to look at all humans as members of the same society, regardless of class, each with a right to search for his happiness in his own way.

The New Lanark community was of course a controlled environment, benevolent in a patriarchal way. The more radical wing of the search for equality in the early nineteenth century was the Chartist and the Trade Union movement, and also the Cooperative Movement founded in 1820. All were politically motivated, though the Cooperative Societies worked entirely through the market system. All were opposed to a greater or lesser extent to the capitalist and class system, and all these three movements sprang from the traumas and suffering inherent in industrialisation and represented the growing power of the working class. Their intentions were to force greater equality between men in society. Trade Unions were made legal by the Combination Acts of 1824 and 1825. The Chartists presented three great petitions to Parliament in 1839, 1842 and 1848, demanding universal manhood suffrage, abolition of the property qualifications for Members of Parliament, and annual elections; to no avail of course.

Later in the nineteenth century, a most articulate branch of socialism, which exists to this day, the Fabian Society developed, whose aim was from the beginning to work towards a more equal society through gradual and reformist methods. It contained, particularly at its most influential period in the late nineteenth to early twentieth century, a dazzling array of articulate writers and speakers. It was actually set up in 1884 in London, and rapidly drew in many influential socialist-inclined figures. These included Edward Carpenter, George Bernard Shaw, H.G.Wells, Graham Wallace, William Morris, R.H.Tawney, Keir Hardie, Hilaire Belloc, Richard Titmuss and of course Sidney and Beatrice Webb.

The heart of the 'story' told by socialism is of a society where the gross inequalities of income and property inherent in our very hierarchical society, are banished – or, at least, greatly modified. Karl Marx, of course, who will be discussed in a later chapter, advocated a forceful end to the injustices which were only too obvious (and still are) in a capitalist system. The Fabian movement, whose name was taken from a Roman emperor famous for his tardiness, thought the change would be more likely to come about by incremental means: by modifying the capitalist system by welfare benefits, taxes and economic engineering whilst still living in it. This approach, which of course was proposed by middleclass, well educated and largely prosperous people, was frequently criticised of doing the opposite of what was aimed at – ie. creating a more equal society in a somewhat less capitalist economic system – by, on the contrary, making capitalism liveable for many more people and thereby perpetuating its existence.

Most of the members had a considerable interest in the characteristics and quality of human nature. Graham Wallace (1858-1932), for instance believed that in the great society held as a vision for the reformers, there must be harmony between human nature and the new society. He was one of the first political thinkers to be interested in Freud and the nature of unconscious impulses: Sigmund Freud's *Interpretation of Dreams* came out in 1899. He was however more optimistic about human nature than Freud and truly hoped for a significant harmony between individual people and the social world. He was also interested in William James's work and his *Principles of Psychology*, accepting that people are both rational and deeply steeped in unconscious material. He grew to believe that any new vision must be wider than Fabians, which is essentially reformative.

Several of the members of the Fabians Society had considerable experience of society outside the bourgeois milieu. Edward Carpenter, openly homosexual, was attracted to working class life and people, where he found happiness and simplicity he felt was unknown to wealthier folk. Replying to birthday congratulations in his later years, he wrote to the Trades Union Congress meeting in Hull: "from the giddy height of my eightieth birthday, I wish to thank the many friends who have on this occasion sent me their message of love and good will....The world, I should say, is all right, or would be all right if people in it...had a grain of real belief in the actual and bed-rock fact of their common dependence on each other.....If this is not a Mad Hatter's tea-party, I don't know what is! I can only say that this sad and foolish tangle is our inheritance from the Commercial Age, and the sooner we can pass out of that age into the age of Common Sense and the real Common Life, the better."[5]

The great scholar R.H.Tawney, who like several others of the group including the Webbs, and later, Virginia Woolf, taught in adult education classes including the East End of London and Manchester, was drawn to the people he found there: "he discovered....that ordinary folk were as capable and virtuous as those who in the name of economic freedom, ruled industry and thereby ruled the 'hands' which stoked the furnaces and worked the looms". These socialist writers, instead of using soldiers, wealthy landowners, lawyers, rulers, as Machiavelli and Hobbes had done, as a template for their understanding of human nature, went further and deeper into society and came up with different conclusions: that human beings varied throughout society in ability and generosity.

However, the rigid inequalities of capitalism were obvious to all, and weren't about to change. Hilaire Belloc wrote a witty comment on the class system in1896 called *'The Justice of the Peace'*

Distinguish carefully between these two,
     This thing is yours, the other thing is mine.
You have a shirt, a brimless hat, a shoe
     And half a coat. I am the Lord benign
Of fifty hundred acres of fat land
     To which I have a right. You understand?

I have a right because I have, because,
    Because I have – because I have a right.
Now be quite calm and good, obey the laws,
    Remember your low station, do not fight
Against the goad, you know, it pricks
    Whenever the ungodly demon kicks.

I do not envy you your hat, your shoe.
    Why should you envy me my small estate?
It's fearfully illogical in you
    To fight with economic force and fate.
Moreover, I have got the upper hand,
    And mean to keep it. Do you understand?

Against the obduracy of this position, inflexibly and stubbornly inbuilt into the psychology of the middle and upper classes, as well as into many workingclass people, as well as into the economic and social structure of the whole society, the vision of change seemed, and was, extremely unlikely to be fulfilled. Sidney and Beatrice Webb, believing in incremental change, took what Bernard Shaw called "this inevitable, but sordid, slow, reluctant and cowardly path to justice" because, as Shaw himself had come to admit, it was the only alternative to an apocalyptic "one great stroke to set Justice on her rightful throne". Shaw went on to say that perhaps cautious and gradual change was necessary in Victorian England, since any transition to socialism could not "be crammed into any Monday afternoon, however sanguinary…Demolishing a Bastille with seven prisoners in it is one thing: demolishing one with fourteen million prisoners is quite another."[6] There are frequent comments among the Fabians that they were living in a hopelessly rotten society, full of suffering for the poor, but patient work is necessary to change it incrementally.

The social myth of freedom and justice envisioned by the fight for equality – or at least less inequality – seems, and probably is – quite unlikely in possessive individualism and industrialised capitalism; the two systems co-existing as in modern Western societies and within modern political theory, mean there is a constant battle between the two. This battle was bitter, and often literally to the death in nineteenth and early twentieth century England. As Karl Marx astutely said in London in April 1856, "In our days everything seems pregnant with its contrary. Machinery, gifted with the wonderful power of shortening and fructifying human labour, we behold starving and overworking it. The new-fangled sources of wealth, by some strange weird spell, are turned into sources of want.....at the same pace that mankind masters nature, man seems to become enslaved to other men or to his own infamy."[7]

Today, we can also see the danger of 'mastering nature', the extraordinary damage that has been done to the land and the planet by industrialisation and the search for wealth: so the contraries are multiplied and made infinitely more complex.

Now the search for economic equality has gone beyond England and the West and applies across the globe. Societies as well as classes and individuals search for more justice in economic terms. Disparities are even more extreme – between the 2 dollars a day, or less, of poverty common to many societies, and the luxury, unexampled in human history, enjoyed by the rich throughout the world.

References

1. Gerrard Winstanley: *The New Law of Righteousness.* 1649
2. Op.cit. p 44
3. Hampton, Christopher: *A radical reader; the struggle for change in England 1381-1914.* Penguin Books. 1984. p189.
4. Owen, Robert: *New View of Society* p22
5. Tsuzuki, Chushichi: *Edward Carpenter 1844-1929: Prophet of Human Fellowship.* Cambridge University Press.1980. p189

6. MacKenzie, Norman and Jeanne: *The First Fabians.* Quartet Books. 1979. p109
7. Hampton op.cit p535

Chapter Five

The Inherently Competitive Nature of Existence?

Organic life beneath the shoreless waves
Was born and nurs'd in Ocean's pearly caves;
First forms minute, unseen by spheric glass,
More in the mud, or pierce the watery mass;
These, as successive generations bloom,
New powers acquire, and larger limbs assume;
Whence countless groups of vegetation spring,
And breathing realms of fin, and feet, and wing.

The Temple of Nature. 1802
Erasmus Darwin.

Erasmus Darwin was the grandfather of Charles. Two generations before Charles he too was preoccupied, in his prolific writings, with the creative power and ongoing life of the earth. The poem above was the thoughtful educated eighteenth, just into nineteenth, century view of creation. Nearly sixty years later, Charles produced his *Origin of Species* in 1859, one of the most influential and significant books – and stories, a great myth – of creation, process and extinction in history, which radically questioned the untroubled contemplation of the eighteenth century view. Charles Darwin's story and what has been made of it by his followers began in political thought and has heavily influenced political understanding to this day.

When we were teaching political philosophy at Brunel University, I wanted to include Charles Darwin in the list of political philosophers. *The Origin of Species* is a truly philosophical book, most fundamentally concerned with power, and enormously influential in the world ever since. Social Darwinism, which sprang from it, contained several of the devils that kept Darwin awake for many nights whilst he contemplated publishing his work. It is ironic that such a thoughtful, responsible, deeply caring and hardworking man unintentionally, yet also with painful doubts, brought forward a theory that has had so many social unexpected side-effects up to the present. He didn't write as a political philosopher but as an excellent scientist. However, it could be argued that his work has deeply affected political thinking – as well as religious and scientific understanding – ever since that time.

The students we taught reckoned that Darwin was one step too far in the slightly unusual 'Political Philosophy' course we taught and he was never included. But I have researched and written on Darwin ever since. It is clear that his work is a pivotal political influence in our social as well as religious understanding, at both a conscious and unconscious level, in our world today. He is definitely part of the story we tell ourselves about power, who we are as humans and the nature of society and the world we inhabit.

It was the work of Thomas Malthus, an economist and clergyman, producing his Essay on the *Principles of Population* in 1798, who profoundly – some few, a minority, would say disastrously - influenced both Charles Darwin – and also Alfred Russel Wallace, a fellow scientist – in the scientific story that they came to tell. Darwin wrote in his *Voyage of the Beagle*, "In October 1838, that is, fifteen months after I had begun my systematic enquiry, I happened to read for amusement 'Malthus on Population', and being well prepared to appreciate the struggle for existence which everywhere goes on, from long continued observation of the habits of plants and animals, it at once struck me that under these circumstances favourable variations would tend to be preserved, and unfavourable ones destroyed. The result of this would be formation of new species."[1] Wallace made the same connection twenty years later, in 1858, battling in Papua New Guinea with malaria and the same issue as Darwin's: how do new species arise? He wrote, ".....one day something brought to my recollection Malthus's *'Principles of Population'*, which I had read about twelve years before. I thought of his clear exposition of the 'positive checks to increase' – disease, accidents, war and famine – which keep down the population of savage races to so much lower an average than that of more civilised peoples. It then occurred to me that these causes or their equivalents are constantly acting in the case of animals also; and as animals usually breed much quicker than does mankind, the destruction every year from these causes must be enormous in order to keep down the number of each species, since they evidently do not increase regularly from year to year, as otherwise the world long ago have been densely crowded with those that breed most quickly. Vaguely thinking over the enormous and constant destruction which this implied, it occurred to me to ask the question, Why do some die and some live? And the answer was clearly, that on the whole the best fitted live....Then it flashed upon me that this self-acting process would necessarily *improve the race,* because in every generation the inferior would inevitably be killed off and the superior would remain - that is, *the fittest would survive....* The more I thought over it the more I became convinced that I had at length found the long-sought-for law of nature that solved the problem of origin of species."[2] It was then Wallace's famous letter containing this theory sent to Darwin that propelled both into publication in 1859 and the initiation of their particular take on the theory of Evolution.

Why was Thomas Malthus's book written and what was he proposing in his book?

Malthus wrote his book as a riposte to his father Daniel Malthus, who espoused the radical French thinkers Rousseau and Condorcet, and the English William Godwin. They optimistically believed human society at the end of the eighteenth century was on the path to perfection, with its new science, art, technology. Godwin's book on this subject Enquiry *Concerning Social Justice* was published in 1793.

Thomas Malthus's book in reply to Godwin's book was the *Essay on the Principle of Population*. He disagreed with his father and with Godwin's optimistic sentiments. It was quickly written and to the point, and came out in 1798.

He immediately states the question at the beginning of Chapter 1, asking "whether man shall henceforth start forwards with accelerated velocity towards illimitable and hitherto unconceived improvement; or be condemned to a perpetual oscillation between happiness and misery, and after every effort remain still at an immeasurable distance from the wished-for goal". He of course argues that the second possibility is the more likely by far.

Malthus states his premises: - i) that food is necessary for people and ii) 'that the passion between the sexes is necessary, and will remain nearly at its present state'. But the problem is that food resources increase only arithmetically and the human population, when unchecked in its 'passion', increases in a geometric ratio. He was very aware that at the beginning of the nineteenth century there was evidence from the newly implemented censuses, that the population was increasing rapidly: this was subsequently substantiated by the 1831 census which showed there were, unbelievably to people at that time, twenty-four million people in Britain, a doubling from the twelve million that were calculated in 1801. This growth was related to the movement of large sections of the population from the country to the town with industrialisation. The factors that kept the population down at all adequately were high levels of infant mortality, poverty, disease, war and famine, in both town and country.

In Malthus's view, though poor people suffered through these afflictions, that was a necessary evil – workhouses should be harsh, not comfortable, so people feared going there. Then they might take voluntary action to check their own birthrate. Malthus was very pessimistic that the lot of the majority of the population could improve: "the principle argument of this essay tends to place in a strong point of view the improbability that the lower classes of people in any country should ever be sufficiently free from want and labour to attain any high degree of intellectual improvement."[3] In other words, there was inherently a war of classes in industrialised society, where the benefit of the wealthy meant the further impoverishment of the many which could but should not be alleviated; a war about resources where every man, or at least every class, was potentially an enemy of every other. But those who survived and flourished in this combative situation would be the most healthy, and probably the most wealthy.

Malthus's work came to be seen by some as a textbook of capitalist ideology. "It is very convenient to think that poverty was due to an 'inevitable' tendency for the population always to be greater than the available food supply, so that the poor were always those upon whom the 'positive checks' were acting". (4), Some of the guilt felt by middleclass people in society could be assuaged by the assumption that the inequalities were inevitable. Malthus's book was indeed very popular, and influenced thought in several sections of society.

It was the aspect of 'struggle for existence' that Wallace and Darwin recognised as the phenomenon they were deeply familiar with in nature, and which spoke to them both in Malthus's book. Darwin wrote, "Nothing is easier than to admit in words the truth of the universal struggle for life, or more difficult – or at least I have found it so – than constantly to bear this conclusion in mind.......We behold the face of nature bright with gladness, we often see superabundance of food; we do not see, or we forget, that the birds that are idly singing round us mostly live on insects or seeds and are thus constantly destroying life; or we forget how largely these songsters, or their eggs, or their nestlings, are destroyed by birds and beasts of prey......There is no exception to the rule that every organic being naturally increases at so high a rate, that if not destroyed, the earth would soon be covered by the progeny of a single pair....It is the doctrine of Malthus applied with manifold force to the whole animal and vegetable kingdoms."[5] But Darwin's and Wallace's application is of struggle for food and resources **between** species, whereas Malthus was writing about the struggle for resources **within** one species. The enormous difference is that the modern human race, a single species, has no predator outside itself: it is only within the species that there is much killing especially in wars and oppression. The context and the arguments are just not the same. The analogy was attractive but misleading. However their use of Malthus's analysis made *Origin of Species* a politically significant book – and applied capitalist principles, directly and unfortunately, to our understanding of the whole Creation.

Not surprisingly, Karl Marx made a similar point in a letter to Engels written on 18 June 1862. He writes, "....Darwin, who I have looked up again, amuses me when he says he is applying the 'Malthusian ' principle also to plants and animals, as if with Mr Malthus the whole point was not that he does not apply the theory to plants and animals but only to human beings – and with geometrical progression – as opposed to plants and animals. It is remarkable how Darwin recognises among beasts and plants his English society with its division of labour, competition, opening up of new markets, 'inventions', and the Malthusian 'struggle for existence. It is Hobbes' *bellum omnium contra omnes* ...."

Therefore, *The Origin of Species* was quickly seen as having enormous political, as well as scientific and religious, implications. It was remembered that Malthus's book *Essay on Population* which was part of its inspiration had been written as a refutation of Godwin's *Enquiry concerning Political Justice* .It was the subject of enormous controversy, and has been ever since.

The dispute around the *Origin* was increased by both Thomas Huxley, an authoritative biologist and anthropologist, and Herbert Spencer, a sociologist, among many others in the furore that followed its publication. Spencer was the author of the phrase 'survival of the fittest' to apply to Darwin and Wallace's theory of evolution which was a phrase not originally used by Darwin. He was a philosopher working towards the evolution of a 'higher' human society, a higher race of mankind. He supported laissez-faire capitalism and competition which he saw as pushing society into new way of being through strong individual effort, and evolution into generating a racial and social hierarchy. This could be aided by the movement towards 'social Darwinism', as the political ramifications of the evolutionary theory came to be known.

Thomas Huxley almost immediately became a supporter of Darwin's theory in 1859, being known as 'Darwin's bulldog'. He later wrote "....from the point of view of the moralist, the animal world is on about the same level as a gladiator's show. The creatures are fairly well treated, and set to fight; whereby the strongest, the swiftest and the cunningest live to fight another day. The spectator has no need to turn his thumb down, as no quarter is given......"[6] He also believed that what was true of animals also included primitive man. I suppose that in both of these examples he is referring to fights usually between members of different species for food.

He also referred back to the seventeenth century Civil Wars....."life was a continuous free fight, and beyond the limited and temporary relations of the family, the Hobbesian war of each against all was the normal state of existence."[7] This conflict is of course between members of the same species. But is difficult to see how killing and competition between members of the same species can be legitimately applied to the killing of one species by another for food.

The influences of Social Darwinism have spread politically and socially from the nineteenth into the twentieth century, both in Europe and America. It is arguable that it has affected socialism and liberalism in Britain as well as conservatism. It supports the view that competition is inherent in the social actions of the human race, and that this can lead to greater health in society. It tended to rank the "fittest" against the less fit, in terms of race, class, educational background. It particularly ranked societies into "higher" and "lower", a tendency seen vividly in early anthropology.

Darwin himself saw a role for both individual and tribal struggle in the evolution of man and feared that the relaxation of selection in civilised communities could be harmful to the race. In America in particular, Darwinian theories were seen to justify highly competitive markets and businesses. Nations, particularly European and North American nations, could see themselves as superior, and justified in running the world, conquering empires and imposing their culture on others.

The most extreme form of social Darwinism was eugenics. Darwin's cousin, Francis Galton, argued that the proportion of people in modern societies was becoming most unbalanced between the numbers of 'fit' and non-fit', and the state would have to play a more active role in controlling the proportions. Too many poor people were having too many children. He wrote a book *Hereditary Genius* in 1869 advocating both 'positive eugenics' – encouraging intelligent wealthier (it was assumed that the two went together) people to have more children: and 'negative eugenics', trying to restrict the number of children being born to less intelligent poorer people of 'inferior' race. Eugenics Societies were set up in Britain and America in the first decade of the twentieth century. Thirty years on, eugenics was a prime factor in the Nazi party in Germany to horrendous effect in the Holocaust and other similar genocides.

There have always been strong protests against Social Darwinian theories. The first really articulate reply came from a fellow scientist, a Russian zoologist and geographer called Prince Peter Kropotkin (1842-1921). Kropotkin attributed the concept of 'Mutual Aid' – the title of his subsequent book - to Professor Kessler who in a lecture in 1880 spoke of mutual aid being of far more significance in the lives of living creatures than the law of mutual struggle. Charles Darwin had himself written about aid within species in his book *The Descent of Man*, he "had argued that the fittest are not the physically strongest, nor the cunningest, but those who learn to combine so as to mutually support each other, strong and weak alike for the welfare of the community.......the term (mutual struggle) which originated from the narrow Malthusian conception of competition between one and all, thus lost its narrowness in the mind of one (Darwin) who knew Nature."[8]

Kropotkin's book *Mutual Aid*, published first in 1902, offers many hundreds of examples of aid animals give to each other, and their ubiquitous sociability in many species – and even between species. In mammals, he writes "the first thing that strikes us is the overwhelming numerical predominance of social species over the few carnivores which do not associate. The plateaus, the Alpines tracts, and the Steppes of the Old and New World are stocked with herds of deer, antelopes, gazelles, fallow deer, buffaloes, wild goats and sheep, all of which are sociable animals."[9] Males who fight for mates do not usually kill each other. He ends the chapter: "Don't compete! – competition is always injurious to the species, and you have plenty of resources to avoid it! That is the *tendency* of nature, not always realised in full, but always present."[10]

In his third chapter he examines "mutual aid among savages", and from the beginning mentions Hobbes and his pessimistic views. The band rather than the family has been the main organising unit for humans through most of their history, he maintains, looking to nineteenth century studies and to anthropology. He maintains the "Eskimo life is based upon communism,"[11] and murder is unknown among most early peoples. He devotes a large part of the book to communities in medieval cities, and in cultures prior to those which are capitalist. His conclusion is that love and sociability rather than conflict between living creatures is predominant even to this day. If it wasn't most species would become extinct.

The conflicts around the implications of the theory of evolution – and the theory itself – have continued to this day. It is interesting that Darwin and Wallace diverged in the rest of their lives over the political connotations. Each retained an enormous respect for the other, but were wary of each other's different convictions about the meaning of their joint work – "I hope you have not murdered too completely your own and my child" wrote Darwin to Wallace after Wallace's book *The Malay Archipelago* was published in 1869.

Wallace himself became a socialist, a believer in a universal spirit, and a supporter of indigenous peoples against what he came to see as the inferior morality of the 'civilised' world. Darwin, a much more conservative man, and a religious doubter, found this painful: "I differ from you, and I am very sorry for it" he wrote to Wallace shortly afterwards. Wallace continued to grapple with issues around meaning until his death at the age of 90 in 1913. He had visited the ecologist John Muir at Yosemite in 1888 and loved the magnificence of the grandest experience of the natural world there. Love of the magnificence of nature was fundamentally where Darwin and Wallace were at one in spirit.

References

1. *Voyage of the Beagle*
2. Raby, Peter: *Alfred Russell Walace, A life.* Chatto and Windus. 2001 pp131/2
3. Malthus, T: *An Essay on the Principle of Population.* Oxford

University Press. 2008. p91

4. Hewetson, John; *Introductory Essay, Mutual Aid and Social Evolution* to Kropotkin's *Mutual Aid.* See Note 10 below. pix

5. Darwin, Charles: *Origin of Species by Means of Natural Selection, or the preservation of favoured races in the struggle for life.* Penguin Books. 1985 pp115/17

6. Huxley, Thomas, cited in Hewetson, John, op.cit. pxi

7. Huxley, Thomas, cited in Hewetson, John, op.cit. pxi

8. Darwin, Charles: *The Descent of Man*

9. Kropotkin, Peter: *Mutual Aid: a Factor of Evolution.* Freedom Press 1987 p47

10. Op.cit. p73

11. Op. cit. p89.

Chapter Six

The free human being suppressed by society and to be liberated by conscious awareness.

I wander thro' each charter'd street,
Near where the charter'd Thames does flow,
And mark in every face I meet
Marks of weakness, marks of woe.

In every cry of every Man,
In every infant's cry of fear,
In every voice, in every ban,
The mind-forg'd manacles appear.

How the chimney-sweeper's cry
Every black'ning Church appals;
And the hapless soldier's sigh
Runs in blood down Palace walls.

But most through midnight streets I hear
How the youthful Harlot's curse
Blasts the new born Infant's tear,
And blights with plagues the Marriage hearse.

William Blake
Keynes, *Complete writings.* K216

The brilliant and heartfelt poems of Blake produced through his long creative life 1757-1827 are not only spiritual and uniquely imaginative, but also political. He was protesting at the society created by capitalism and the industrial revolution in England, by the inequality and inhumane conditions in which most people lived throughout their lives, and also at the ideas which had caused such a society to exist; the ideas, as quoted above, of John Locke in politics and Isaac Newton in science.

There have been, through this four hundred long period of history, many voices raised, often perilously, against the world brought into being partly by the political thinkers examined in the first chapters of this book. These questioning voices included specifically other more radical political thinkers. Some of these thinkers have been discussed in Chapter Four – Winstanley, Owen, some of the early socialists. Other philosophers we taught on our Political Ideas course were, in the eighteenth century, Jean-Jacques Rousseau, Thomas Paine and Mary Wollstonecraft : in the nineteenth century, Karl Marx of course, and Peter Kropotkin already mentioned in the last chapter, and in the twentieth century, Mohandas Gandhi. In this chapter I can only write quite sparsely on such a number of disparate people.

Jean Jacques Rousseau was born in Geneva in 1712: his mother died a week after he was born, and he had an interrupted childhood, running away to France when he was fifteen. However, he had long periods of happiness in his life (as well as deep despair) and basically regarded himself as a happy man. He developed a gradual self-awareness in his eventful life, and is different from most of the philosophers considered so far, in that towards the end of his life he wrote his books *Confessions, Reveries of the Solitary Walker,* and *Dialogues*, reflecting on himself and his place in the world: a rare self-reflexive political philosopher. His more theoretical books concerning the nature of society, politics, inequality and education were produced earlier. He died in 1778.

He begins Chapter 1 of his famous *The Social Contract or Principles of Political Right* with the striking words "Man is born free; and everywhere he is in chains. One thinks himself the master of others, and still remains a greater slave than they". He was concerned not only with the phenomenon of inequality but also with its deeply political nature, asking himself the question (as he writes in Book IX of *The Social Contract*), "What is the nature of the form of government fitted to create a people that will be most virtuous, the most enlightened and the wisest, in fact the best, taking this word in its widest sense?" This is the question of this book, and one which is ever more urgent in our day. He makes the interesting point above that our political and economic system imprisons not only the poor but also the rich and powerful by crushing us into set roles so very few of us are truly free.

The books Rousseau wrote were inspired by a vision he had in 1749, when he was in his 30s; in this he perceived the contradictions of the social system. In a letter he said, "oh, if I could have written a quarter of what I saw and felt under that tree, how clearly I should have brought to view all the contradictions of the social system, how powerfully I should have laid bare all the abuses of our institutions, how simply I would have demonstrated that man is naturally good, and it is only through these institutions that men become evil!"[1]

His view, contrary to that of Hobbes and Locke, is that people were much freer in earlier natural societies. They were more solitary, less greedy, healthier, and in general harmless to themselves, their social groups and the natural world around them. In fact, he believed the human race in a state of nature to be innocent, less different from all other animals, and living in a more benign world. The problem was that people have an urge for improvement and begin to 'civilise'. They also learn a fear of death in anticipation of its inevitability. And they learned to see the meaning of 'good' as opposed to natural – which of course is the subject of Genesis in the Bible: as soon as you can see good, you perceive the possibility of evil, a point made at the root of Taoist thinking. And even empathy and compassion can work two ways, as these qualities can provide a refined edge to evil, an enjoyment at the suffering of others. He makes the interesting statement that "in reality, the source of all these difference is, that the savage lives within himself, while social man lives constantly outside himself, and only knows how to live in the opinion of others, so that he seems to receive the consciousness of his own existence merely from the judgment of others concerning him."[2]

He specifically criticised earlier thinkers, particularly Hobbes, in their view of human nature: "every one of them...constantly dwelling on wants, avidity, oppression, desires and pride, has transferred to the state of nature ideas that were contained in society: so that, in speaking of the savage, they described the social man." Indeed Hobbes specifically admitted that himself, as I mention in Chapter 2.

Rousseau's view was that every creature born into the world sought its own perfectibility and cited Aristotle for this opinion: he believed the human race could be in the same category as all other beings, if it only woke up.

His views of freedom did not extend to women. "The relative duties of the two sexes are not, and cannot be, equally rigid. When woman complains of the unjust inequality, which man has imposed on her, she is wrong; this inequality is not a human institution, or at least it is not the work of prejudice but of reason; that one of the sexes to whom nature has entrusted the children must answer for it to the other"[3]. These remarks are most painfully ironic when we learn that Rousseau and his wife Therese gave away the five children born to them at birth to an orphanage.

Rousseau is famous for his depiction of 'the noble savage' and the original wholesomeness of the baby. "Everything is good when it leaves the hands of the Creator. It degenerates in the hands of man.....he mutilates his dog, his horse, his slave.........he wants nothing to be made as nature made it, not even man; he breaks him in like a horse, and makes him conform to his taste like a tree in the garden". This is the first paragraph of *Emile*, his interesting book on the education of boys and men, and his proposals for a totally reformed education system.

Rousseau thought that there is evidence that earlier societies were far less oppressive than the Europe he inhabited in the eighteenth century. The corruption comes from the institution of property, which divides society into the rich and the poor. All society becomes false and things and people become valued for their appearance, not for their reality; servility becomes endemic.

If people were not servile, they would be able to take a full part in the political life of the society. He advocated full participatory government for men, through a process he called the General Will. Then both people and society would have a chance of reaching the potential he felt was available to the human race.

Thomas Paine (1757-1809) and
Mary Wollstonecraft (1759-1797)

I have linked these two writers together because Paine brought out his *Rights of Man* in 1791, and Mary Wollstonecraft her *Vindication of the Rights of Women* in response in 1792. Both had international connections, particularly with France and the French Revolution of 1789, and Tom Paine with America and its severance from the British Empire and its new founding Constitution. And both of course supported the new idea of individual rights: they were individualists but they were also supporting fiercely the notion of more equality – or at least less inequality. Mary met William Blake in the 1780s, and she and Tom Paine knew each other. Paine had a Quaker background. Wollstonecraft married the anarchist William Godwin in 1797, but died in childbirth that same year: her daughter, also Mary, eventually married Percy Shelley and it was as Mary Shelley that she wrote the brilliant horror story *Frankenstein*. Both Wollstonecraft and Paine shared the conviction that humans were potentially good: they were both more liberal than socialist, in modern terms.

Tom Paine's first book was called *Common Sense,* written for the American public in a very straightforward style, and selling 120,000 copies in its first three months. He made the interesting distinction between society and government: "society is produced by our wants, and government by our wickedness; the former promotes our happiness **positively** by uniting our affections, the latter **negatively** by restraining our vices". He was against monarchy and titles, which he thought ridiculous and childish. Law should be king "and there ought to be no other".

His major book, *The Rights of Man,* was in answer to Edmund Burke's attack on the French Revolution. Parts of it are remarkably modern. He advocated universal public education; childrens' allowances and old age pensions to begin at 50 (though of course life expectancy was much shorter 250 years ago); progressive income tax. He was opposed to government being determined by tradition - by past generations – and said that power should be in the hands of the living, not dominated by the dead. Paine thought modern societies should offer people better natural rights than they could have obtained previously, not worse. As the French Revolution had proclaimed (though didn't manage to implement), there should be a Universal Right of conscience, not just tolerance, with freedom of speech. He thought England ought to have a written Constitution to proclaim these rights, as the newly-found America was carrying out in their own Constitution. He spoke for religious toleration: "why may we not suppose that the great Father of all is pleased with a variety of devotion?" He believed there would be a new start, with the promising beginnings in the French and American rebellions, and with the memory in Britain of the Civil War of the 1640s, but he died a disappointed man, when all the hopes he had either came to nothing or were tarnished by the violence produced by pressures for change in France and the existence and treatment of slaves in America.

Mary Wollstonecraft responded to Rousseau and Paine by writing the first major book proposing specifically that women should have equal legal and political rights as men, which were denied by Rousseau and largely ignored by Paine. William Blackstone, the authority on British Law in his *Commentaries on the English Constitution* of 1758 demonstrated the 'civil death' experienced by women at marriage when they lost their own legal rights to their husbands: "by marriage, the husband and wife are one person in law; that is, the very being or legal existence of the woman is suspended during the marriage or at least is incorporated and consolidated into that of the husband; under whose wing, protection and cover, she performs everything." She could hold no property in her own right, or have any separate claim over her children. She certainly had no economic independence, and if the 'wing, protection and cover' cited failed to protect, she had no redress. She of course she had no vote, of whatever class she came.

Wollstonecraft, like Paine, wrote with some style and very directly. She declared in her Introduction and Dedication that she "loudly demands(ed) JUSTICE for one-half of the human race". She demanded serious education for women, rather than the kind of teaching-to-please that middleclass women received which considered "females rather as women than human creatures": rather women should have the access to an education which would enable them to "unfold their faculties" as men could. "Are women meant to have no souls of their own, but only to be there for the benefit of men?"

She interestingly commented that many young girls are often full of energy – they can be 'a romp'. But this disappears as they enter the education that is offered them and lose all challenge to their wits if they are middleclass: they would of course have severe challenges if they were working women, but of a desperate rather than facilitating kind. This lack of challenge puts them into the same category as the rich of both sexes who "have acquired all the vices and follies of civilisation, and missed the useful fruit."[4]. Power corrupts the powerful as well as oppressing the victims of power.

Her summary is about the need for society to be conducted to enable all to lead fulfilling lives: this she perceived to be the aim of law and of politics. She ended her book by writing "confined….. in cages like the feathered race, they (middleclass women) have nothing to do but plume themselves, and stalk with mock majesty from perch to perch. It is true that they are provided with food and raiment, for which they neither toil of spin; but health, liberty and virtue are given in exchange".

Wollstonecraft wrote her book in about 6 weeks, in the middle of a busy life. It was a protest rather than a political tract for implementation in law or the political system. She was rightly dubious that any specific change would be effected by it – and indeed, society as it ended the nineteenth century became less sympathetic to the openly radical major protests of the eighteenth century in France and America. However, the book continues to make a good read, and is written with true spirit, thought and feeling, speaking to later generations.

Karl Marx 1818-1883

Marx of course was writing about what he also called 'alienation' which is the keynote of Wollstonecraft's complaint. Property and the system of capitalism he saw as the expression of man's alienated life: this drastically affected a working man's life. He wrote that for workers, "his own life is an object to him" – in other words, not expressing his own nature, but being imposed on from outside by the system. It alienates from man his own body: nature is exterior to him: and so is his intellect and his human essence. Private property is the result of alienated labour.

Marx here refers us to the implementation of John Locke's proposals in the *Second Treatise* which were successfully applied in the 150 years between the two writers. Locke had been analysing what was actually happening in society, but by putting the capitalist model into words, he strengthened it and made it most transportable to other lands. In Marx's view, the alienation of workers as opposed to middleclass people, was so strong as to create a whole working-class. He wrote in *The Eighteenth Brumaire of Louis Napoleon*, "in so far as millions of families live under economic conditions of existence that separate their mode of life, their interests, and their culture from those of the other classes and put them in a hostile opposition to the latter, they form a class." This class system is directly related to the means of production and the ownership of property. Marx and Engels proclaimed in *The Communist Manifesto* of 1848 , "the history of all hitherto existing society is the history of class struggles".

He was influenced by the evolutionary thinking so character-istic of the nineteenth century to predict that the next evolu-tionary stage inevitable to capitalism would be the violent revolution of the working classes in advanced industrialised societies. A subsequent dictatorship of that class would eventually lead to a classless and entirely democratic non-capitalist society. Of course, though he regarded himself as a scientist, this is a prophetic message and myth which did not subsequently work out historically according to his plan. Communism has been enormously powerful in the world, but the first country, Russia, to espouse it was a country of serfs and not highly industrialised at all; the biggest nation to which it has appealed has been China, which at that time was largely agricul-tural with relatively little industry.

However, the strength of Marxism or Communism has been in its energetic and often effective critique of capitalism, over the 160 years of its existence. The programme of the Manifesto included the abolition of property in land, a heavy progressive income tax, abolition of all rights of inheritance, centralisation of credit in the state, equal liability of all to labour, free education for all children, and the eventual abolition of classes. There should be full employment of all citizens. These proposals have affected all socialist and radical thinking in subsequent years.

Karl Marx had early in his life been heavily influenced by Hegel's work. Both believed that people in the course of their lives, create themselves, largely through their work. This was why the nature of work mattered so much – it was about the fulfilment of human potential. Marx was always searching for a real transformation of society "whose moral aspect would be the re-acquisition by man of his natural qualities, a rehabilitation of himself as a social being liberated from enslaving alienations."[5]. Marx was searching for a world, as he explained in the *Economic and Social Manuscripts* of 1844, where people could live fully as creatures gifted with many senses and intelligence, fully experiencing society, the world and Nature. At the root of his protests was a fundamental criticism of capitalist society which destroyed through its institutions the natural potential of the human being.

The final words of the Communist Manifesto are:

"The communists disdain to conceal their views and aims. They openly declare that their ends can be attained only by the forcible overthrow of all existing social conditions. Let the ruling classes tremble at a Communistic revolution. The proletariat have nothing to lose but their chains. They have a world to win. WORKING MEN OF ALL COUNTIRES, UNITE!

References

1. In John Hall: *Rousseau: an introduction to his political philosophy*. Macmillan 1973.
2. Rousseau J-J: *Discourse on Inequality*.
3. Rousseau J-J. *Emile*
4. Wollstonecraft Mary: *Vindication of the Rights of Women*. Penguin Books. 1985. p151
5. Karl Marx: *Selected writings in Sociology and Social Philosophy* ed. T.B.Bottomore & M.Rubel. Penguin 1965 p22

Chapter Seven

Summarising these myths and the issues of consciousness/unconsciousness

"Every man carries heaven and hell with him in this world"

Jacob Boehme (1575-1624)

".....the more men try to dominate life by conscious reason, the more irrational they become."

Alan Watts, *The Meaning of Happiness.*

The conscious debate

In this first section of the book, I have concentrated on writers, political philosophers, who have naturally articulated their experience of the age in which they live from their own historical and personal standpoint. From this experience each has developed a political statement about his or her own reality, and the reality they saw around them. We are all creatures of our own time. From our present point of view, this has resulted in a dialogue, a disputation over time, between the participants. This particular political writing has had an influence, indeed a power, over the world we presently live in because Western economic and political values have become so pervasive throughout the globe, affecting the lives of the vast majority of people living now. Most of this writing has originated in Europe, and indeed much of it in England. English is the most common language used in powerful international organisations such as the United Nations, the World Bank or the Stock Market. The modern world is predominantly capitalist and increasingly global.

Several major themes are run through in the political debates over the five centuries covered in the first part of the book. I tried to chose the most influential and articulate theorists for the course and for this book. All present their own original version of the politics of their time, which is partly unique to them but also picks up the values and forces in their own society – and puts these values into words.

The first and most fundamental theme is the debate about human nature, because on this all other assumptions have to be made. The last centuries in the West have been very fraught and indeed very violent. The earliest writers, Machiavelli and Hobbes, wrote out of their urgent need to understand their tumultuous societies, in Italy and England, in a state of war: and set to work out how order could be brought about. Both looked around them and found a world full of men fighting each other, and came to assume this was how men naturally are: how they are when born. Hobbes' assumption that men are naturally at war with each other is often quoted, to this day. Darwin, Huxley and Spencer were aware of this in working out the theory of evolution. Modern politicians have the words "nasty, brutish and short" immediately to hand about the human condition, as do many others (although those words were actually about a failure to take prudent action which was the subject of Hobbes's comment).

The assumption about the warlike nature of human beings could be asserted with some confidence because it resonated with the notion of Original Sin which was threaded through both the powerful Catholic and the Protestant churches of these centuries – and still is, to this day. I will discuss this point further in the second part of this chapter.

Other theorists had different assumptions. Locke believed that humans are like a sheet of white paper when we are born – yet to be written on. In his view it is the society and particularly education that matters in the development of each person's

73

potential. J.S. Mill, two centuries on, believed in the initial freedom of the individual – men *and* women alike, quite different from Locke's assumptions – but seeing it was the structure of society that created the damaged, violent and suffering world.

It is the protesters throughout the ages who tend to believe that when a child is born, he or she comes perfectly formed from the hands of the Creator if they are Christian, or whole and unique beings if they are not. We are alright at birth. It's what happens afterwards that is the problem. Rousseau believed that the problem of a violent world lies in how humans have constructed 'civilisation' and the pernicious influence of its institutions, of family, marriage, and education in the eighteenth century. Tom Paine believed that all men are formed in the image of God, and had natural rights over their bodies and minds: they are born equal and all people need to be treated with respect: he was a rational Deist and believed people were naturally good. Mary Wollstonecraft heartily and forcefully expressed that the repression of women, one half of the human race, in social society, is the enemy of freedom and human potential. And of course Karl Marx's analysis bitterly blamed capitalism, particularly possessive capitalism, as the repressor of working people, which cut society in half separating those who could possess and those who had no power. The basic radical view over the last six centuries in Europe has been "that all men should be free and of one condition", as Wat Tyler expressed it. But this is not the root lying at much of the politics we have today.

A second big theme, the major phenomenon socially and economically, that has developed over these centuries has been the growth of capitalism. The debate around this is whether each philosopher supported and indeed facilitated the capitalist system or whether he or she rejected it, which is now is an issue for the whole world.

The spirit of capitalism as it developed in the seventeenth century is well described by John Donne, Thomas Hobbes and

John Locke. It assumes competition to be a major element in human nature - at least in male human nature, because that is the presupposition of Hobbes and Locke. It assumes the earth is here as a resource for humans, and that is its sole purpose. It advocates the accumulation of capital, in land, in goods and in money, so as to further great projects. It sees the world as a huge market place, a maker of money and goods, an enrichment of the conditions of living for people. Within the seventeenth and eighteenth centuries, the structure for this enterprise, this new paradigm in Kuhn's terms, was laid down. By the end of the period there were banks, a system of the payment of interest, a stock market for buying and selling, a large place for business in society, and industrialisation, all springing from the scientific and technological knowledge made possible by the wealth that was being created.

The sociologist Max Weber wrote the material for his best selling book *The Protestant Ethic and the Spirit of Capitalism* in 1904-5 (it was then in two articles).

He quotes an American capitalist, Benjamin Ferdinand, of that time, giving something of the flavour of the capitalist spirit:

'Remember that *time* is money. He that can earn ten shillings a day by his labour, and goes abroad, or sits idle, one half of that day, though he spends but sixpence during his diversion or idleness, ought not to reckon *that* the only expense; he has really spent, or rather thrown away, five shillings besides.

Remember, that *credit* is money. If a man lets his money lie in my hands after it is due, he gives me the interest, or as much as I can make of it during that time. This amounts to a considerable sum where a man has good and large credit, and makes good use of it.

Remember, money is of the prolific, generating nature. Money can beget money, and its offspring can beget more, and so on. Five shillings turned is six, turned again is seven and threepence, and so on, till it becomes a hundred pounds. The more of it there is of it, the more it produces at every turning so the profits rise quicker and quicker. (p48)." So you can never get enough of it! As Weber commented then, capitalism means that "man is dominated by the making of money, by acquisition as the ultimate purpose of life". [1]

The wealth capitalism and industrialisation have produced is incontrovertible in 'developed' countries: we presently live comfortably with all the advantages it brings. All conservatives, most liberals and many socialists largely accept the system in rich countries. Marx of course fought it, as do some left-wing socialists. Its force has destroyed much of the earth and her creatures, and many simpler, older, more sustainable ways of living.

Obviously, what most particularly is missing in the assumptions that have been made in the main body of political theory is the Other – those elements not considered by most major political thinkers. Throughout most of these centuries, the people who really mattered were property holders and wealthy men, often aristocrats. Women did not count, unless they were aristocratic, propertied in their own right, or royal. The poorer people were not considered. Universal franchise did not happen in England until 1928. In spite of all the activities of Trade Unions, Chartists and other radical groups in the nineteenth century working men did not get the vote until the Reform Acts of 1884/5, and fully only at the end of the First World War. People in other lands with different cultures from the European were seen as savages, by political thinkers and biologists alike.

Secondly, because from the seventeenth century onwards modern countries have been deeply materialistic, the sense of a more pervasive spiritual reality beyond the rational ordering of institutions has been largely missing, or at least been seen as secondary. This was not so with Hobbes, whose third and fourth main chapters of *Leviathan* were entitled "Of a Christian Commonwealth" and "Of a Kingdom of Darkness", reading quite strangely to a modern eye. But he did not take spiritual factors much into account in his theories because he believed the framework he was advocating was scientific. As science on the one hand and values on the other have increasingly been seen as lying in different realms of human life, a sense of the cosmos was not seen as relevant to his message. The spiritual dimension has been largely irrelevant to politics ever since, with Church and State firmly separate. This division is of course very desirable in general, but it does mean that politics is mainly on a rational rather than a values or metaphysical level: quite one-dimensional.

A third element that could be missed in political writing is self-reflexive awareness on the part of the writer. It is striking, looking at the childhoods of most of the writers, that by and large they had disturbed and we might say extremely deprived childhoods. Most – with the exception of Rousseau – did not write about themselves. It could be argued that most children during the years of capitalism and industrialisation, in the fragile nuclear family, were very vulnerable to ill fortune. We could certainly be quite justified in saying that the political writing we have been looking at came largely out of a conflictful, dangerous world which was so taken for granted as normal for children as well as adults that no consideration as to its psychological effect on the material written was seen to be necessary. Even John Stuart Mill, brought up in middleclass comfort, was force-fed into knowledge by an enormously strict and ambitious father, James Mill.

A most striking omission now, with our present threatening knowledge, is how the earth was seen as resources and open to possession, there for human use. In fact it is difficult to find any questioning of this even in the debate on nature and evolution, though Darwin and Wallace had such a feeling for the earth and its creatures. But reading most political philosophy, it is as though we are reading about a totally separate species, divorced from the millions of others species with which it exists.

There is a larger point here, which is about the dualistic nature of Western thinking. Undoubtedly the world works in opposites, but it is striking in much of the political thinking described, writers come down firmly on one side or another of any argument without reference to the opposite: we are good/they are bad; we are people and can take the earth for granted/it is not counted; adults are important, not children; we are rational beings more particularly if we are men, rich, white.

These lead us easily into the next Section of the book. But first it is interesting to go a bit deeper, and ask about some of the implicit, more fundamental questions it is possible to investigate from the level of the myth-like stories we tell ourselves about the world and what we are doing here.

The unconscious

This was the conscious picture. But more and more of us have learnt, particularly in modern times from depth psychology, that what happens in both individual and social affairs, is conscious and rational only to some extent. We are also driven by forces, both individual and social, of which we are only dimly aware. Philosophers and poets have commented on unconscious forces over the last two to three thousand years at least, in both eastern and western thought: Freud acknowledged this at his seventieth birthday celebrations when he said, "the poets and philosophers before me discovered the unconscious. What I discovered was the scientific method by which the unconscious can be studied." St Augustine, who lived between 354 and 430 C.E. wrote: "Great is the power of memory, exceedingly great. O my God, a spreading limitless room is within me. Who can reach its uttermost depth? Yet it is a faculty of soul. In fact I cannot totally grasp all that I am."[2] And there is an elegant poem at the head of the last chapter in the book by Kabir, the Persian poet living at the end of the Middle Ages, fully perceiving the relationship between the two worlds of consciousness and unconsciousness.

Speaking of the unconscious brings us back to the myths, the stories we tell ourselves privately as well as publicly, referred to in my first chapter. The political philosophers are articulate and bring us words, concepts, rationality, frameworks for action, but beneath all that are enduring ways of knowing in the world which are deeper, wider, more universal. This depth of feeling, instinct, imagination and spirit is most readily expressed in poetry, which is my reason for using poetry throughout the chapters. Kathleen Raine has an interesting phrase, when writing of Shelley's poetry, when she said: "…Shelley understood that the poet, *whose politics are those of eternity*, has for that very reason a responsibility towards the politics of time."[3] Defending Ancient Springs, my italics). The perception of great poets can be nearer to being cleansed, seeing more directly and more deeply into the unconscious, and perhaps into eternity.

The personal unconscious, in the understanding of Carl Jung or Roberto Assagioli who developed psychosynthesis,[4] is that part of ourselves of which we are most aware of in dreams, daydreams, religious experience or any kind of creativity. It has been said that our conscious self is like the tip of the iceberg of our entire being: we can have some awareness of the elements 'under water', so to speak, in many ways, some fleeting, others familiar, but we only understand a relatively small amount of the motivations and qualities of our lives. Some relatively uncon-scious material can be brought quickly to mind – a forgotten name, a scent that reminds you vividly of whole different entire world, some instances can give you coded messages in dreams: at other times, one does something instinctively, quickly, without thinking, as though obeying a sharp personal message, and you realise that action comes from somewhere else. Transpersonal psychology tends to make a distinction between the lower unconscious, which calls on elements in the past, particularly in early childhood, which have been presumably forgotten but which can forcefully affect our lives, and higher unconsciousness – those elements of beauty, love, will, spirit, mystery which may be equally ignored in our materialistic world.

Collectively, all of us living in society, have a shared **collective consciousness** which is cultural and refers to the knowledge we carry of the social world. Cultures of societies differ enormously through time and space, and can carry differences both local and national, relatively stable or relatively fluid. In addition we carry a strong force which is known as **collective unconsciousness**, which Jung in particular has written about. The collective uncon-scious depicts "the human being as a kind of receiver, almost like a television set, that is potentially tuned into...... all the human experience there has been until now. In this vast mass, there are archetypes, forms relevant to the human condition that have appeared in many races and times: the Mother or Father archetype, for instance, the image of the mother or father figure that seems to be carried around by every person regardless of his or her actual experience. We convey this largely unconscious knowledge by myths and fairy stories by religious or sacred symbols, by depiction of forms of Good and Evil"[5].

Jung in his classic book *The Archetypes and the Collective Unconscious* sums up his thesis thus: "In addition to our immediate consciousness, which is of a thoroughly personal nature and which we believe to be the only empirical psyche (even if we tack on the personal unconscious as an appendix), there exists a second psychic system of a collective, universal and impersonal nature which is identical in all individuals. This collective unconscious does not develop individually but is inherited."[6]. However, it seems to me that the even the collective unconscious is modified and changed by personal experience, especially as there are obviously many models , symbols, myths of, say, Good and Evil. It is the duality of good and evil that many of the political philosophers write about: it is the acting-out of the human being that has to be dealt with in society and through the systems of power.

As many writers have conceived of the collective unconscious in modern times, it is concerned with the profoundest issues of time, space, timelessness, existence, God, goodness and evil, meaning: as John Francis Phipps discusses in his book *The Politics of Inner Experience* these deep issues are, in any healthy society at the heart and centre of political and social life. But we in the last few hundred years in the West have separated our knowledge into separate categories, dividing science from religion, person from Universe, feeling from intellect. It is this that the several writers, William James in *Varieties of Religious Experience*, David Bohm in *Wholeness and the Implicate Order*, Rupert Sheldrake in *The Presence of the Past*, question. However, it was Blake who put this understanding most succinctly. He understood the agony of the societies we have created, as he expressed in the poem at the beginning of Chapter Six. He saw the cause as materialism, unwillingness to access spirit in modern societies, an unawareness of the existential and the mysterious. "If the doors of perception were cleansed, everything would appear to man as it is, infinite. For man has closed himself up, till he sees all things through narrow chinks of his cavern"[7]. Blake, a very political poet is conscious of the unconscious aspect of the issues I discussed in the first section – duality, how we understand human nature, awareness and the determination not to be aware, and the violence and the suffering we experience and cause. But he was also aware of Heaven as well as Hell – and as Kabir's poem suggests at the beginning of chapter 15, he believed that human recognition and working through the contraries was the cause of all creation – the holy one silently growing within.

"Without Contraries is no progression. Attraction and

Repulsion, Reason and Energy,

Love and Hate, are necessary to the Human existence.

From these energies spring what the religious call Good and Evil.

Greed is the passive that obeys Reason. Evil is the active springing from Energy.

Good is Heaven. Evil is Hell."

William Blake. *The Marriage of Heaven and Hell*

The conscious and the unconscious together are about the spring of creativity. Separated, they are utterly dangerous. With awareness their meeting is the fount of all the awesome life of the Universe. Jung believed that the human task is to make the unconscious conscious, at every level, personal and collective.

As a corollary, I would like to say something about a story, a dogma, a spiritual decision, that lies dangerous curled up at the heart of Western civilisation and that has affected much of the thinking this book has been discussing, particularly on the nature of human beings. It is the Christian doctrine of Original Sin, which is derived from the Genesis story of The Fall of mankind. This could take a book in itself, and indeed an interesting book *The Fall* by Steven Taylor has recently been published on the subject. Such a spiritual decision can be quickly and consciously related, but the ramifications of this belief spread through the unconscious as well as the conscious of our spiritual world to the present. It is as though it was placed in one of the lower levels of Hell in Dante's *The Divine Comedy*, a place of deep unconsciousness. It is not surprising that the question of the nature of the person is central to political philosophy: the issue has been central through the ages to any story we tell ourselves about who we are.

The actual decision to include Original Sin into the canons of the early Western Church was made at the Council of Carthage in

418 C.E. This account follows that of J.N.D.Kelly's book *Early Christian Gospels* in the chapter on 'Fallen Man and God's Grace'. In the fourth century beliefs about man's fallen state and need for divine help were held, together and contrarily with a dogged belief in free will and responsibility among the thinkers of the time..

The matter was finally disputed at Carthage in 418. Pelagius, a British monk of no particular religious order, represented what then was seen as a creationist stance, which concerned the primacy of unconditional free will and responsibility, though within a framework of morality. Kelly writes, "Since each soul is, as he believed, created immediately by God, it cannot come into the world soiled by original sin transmitted by Adam.....before he begins exercising his will there is only in him what God has created."[9] Pelagius believed that a person could only lead an acceptably good life by strenuous effort, but that such a life was possible even though each person was weak: he had a strong belief in God's majesty. He believed that babies were full of potential when they were born, having God as their creator. However Pelagius and his followers were generally held to have too rosy a view of the possibility of living a wholesome life. Augustine however held that Adam, in spite of his amazingly good fortune of living with all wants satisfied, did fall, entirely from his own fault. This sin was so great that it rebounded on the entire human race: "so Augustine has no doubt of the reality of original sin"[10] He saw that sin as sexual desire is a joint inherited guilt. He wrote, "without God's help we cannot by free will overcome the temptations of this life"[11]. And he believed we are born evil and this has to be eliminated.

At the Council of Carthage, confirmed by Pope Zosimus, the doctrine of Pelagius was outlawed and that of Augustine was adopted by the Western Christian Church, though the Eastern Christian Churches never adopted it and remains to the present in both Catholic and Protestant churches: "there is no health in us", according to the Confession of the Church of England. This assumption needs to be brought to the light of day, cleared into consciousness and deeply questioned. It is usually not related to political thought, but in my view it is forcefully at the heart of it.

References

1. Weber, Max : *The Protestant Ethic and the Spirit of Capitalism.* Unwin Books 1976
2. Ibidem
3. See *A Psychology with a Soul.* Hardy, Jean. p63
4. Whyte L.L. : *The Unconscious before Freud* Julian Friedman 1978 p79
5. Raine Kathleen: *Defending Ancient Springs* Golgonooza Press. p151
6. Hardy Jean: *A Psychology with a Soul.* Woodgrange Press 1996. p32
7. Jung Carl: *The Archetypes and the Collective Unconscious* Routledge 2008 p43
8. Keynes, G: *Complete Writings of William Blake* (and numbering), 154
9. Taylor, Steven: *The Fall.* O-Books 2008
10. Kelly J.N.D. *Early Christian Gospels.* A&C Black. 1985 pp358/9
11. ibid. p363
12. ibid p366

Recognising and responding to the Other

The political philosophy that we have, upon which our present political system is based, was largely developed at a particular period, the sixteenth to the nineteenth century, in Europe: indeed most of it is of English origin. This philosophy is at the heart of liberal and conservative capitalism which has spread throughout the world and is hardly challenged in the West, except by Marxism which is now rarely taken seriously as a basis for modern democratic systems. Isaiah Berlin in his book *Against the Current: Essays in the History of Ideas,* first published in 1955, is one of the few really respected philosophers of modern times to challenge the whole, general caucus of political ideas under which we now live. In his excellent Introduction to Berlin's book, Roger Hausheer underlines this neglect, commenting "the adequacy of our fundamental (political) propositions – how much of our experience they include, how much they leave out, how much they illuminate and how much obscure – should be of central concern to both philosophers and historians of ideas"[1] – and indeed to all the rest of us. Hausheer goes on to write: "these underlying ubiquitous presuppositions, precisely because they are of a high degree of generality and themselves serve as the means whereby we order a very large part – the human part – of our experience, have usually remained submerged and unexamined: the task of the historian of ideas is to try to get outside them, to make them objects of reflection and systematic study, thereby bringing them into the light where they can be openly criticised and evaluated. Many of our values and ideals....will be revealed for what they are: not timeless, objective, unshakeable, self-evident truths derived from the eternal and immutable essence of human nature, but the late and fragile blossoms of a long, untidy, often painful and tragic, but ultimately intelligible historical process of human change."[2]

These reflections directly apply to the ideas I have presented in Part One. There are conflicts within the dialogue, but they do represent a way of seeing the world which spring from an ever changing but deeply related Western culture which has evolved and been played out over perhaps 500 years of our recent history, and which I have briefly examined. They are, in Hausheer's words, the untidy, painful, tragic, and ultimately intelligible presuppositions within which we live.

In my view, our political culture holds in common some or all of the following assumptions in the story they tell of our reality:-

i.   The human world is a male dominated one. The philosophy was overwhelmingly written by men for men, particularly for those men counted as citizens, and largely makes the assumption that men are without question the significant decision makers. Mary Wollstonecraft protested about this in 1792 in *Vindication of the Rights of Women*, but women in England only obtained the vote on the same grounds as men in England in 1928. More than that, the conception of human nature on which the theories are founded is decidedly male and emphasises the warlike nature of man. And many of the writers were swayed by the notion of Progress, of humans being enabled to create a much improved world, using nature but improving on her. Most of the philosophy was written at a time when government was restricted to affluent males and speaks to them in particular.

ii.   This human world was definitely divided into 'us' and 'them'. The rich white man was the template for 'us'. From the early political philosophers onwards, other races and cultures were regarded as the childhood of the human race, definitely inferior, with the white man as being in the van of progress. As Kirkpatrick Sale pointed out in his *The Conquest of Paradise*, it is more than possible that all the millions of peoples conquered by the European invaders from 1492 onwards, in what we came to call America, who had lived there sustainably for thousands of years, had a superior and deeper vision of life than their Western conquerors, who sought only gold and land, and the building of an empire. The assumed superiority of the white man was extended to the conquering of many areas of the world in the eighteenth century onwards, ignoring the deep spiritual philosophy often found in Asia and Africa, and setting out to 'civilise' those regarded as 'natives'. By the beginning of the twentieth century the British Empire covered a quarter of the world and the world's populations. Several European countries had comparable empires.

iii. The political philosophy we live by had, and largely still has, little consideration of the natural world we live in. For most of the writers included in the second section, the human race stood alone and without context. The earth and the millions of other species were ignored by most political philosophers. Even Darwin, who loved the earth and revered the diversity of species, saw his studies largely in relation to 'Man', and eventually the evolution of mankind. Western culture usually counts other animals as non-beings, here for our use: and the earth, as Locke expressed so graphically, as is seen essentially a human possession – an assumption that many American Indians found ludicrous – "how can we *possess* the earth?" they protested, seeing the earth as being the powerful being and humans dependent on her. If we could extend our political vision of ourselves now to include other animals and the whole of creation around us, an immense change indeed, what new story would we need to develop?

iv. The political story told in Part One is mostly secular and rational. This is not to say that many political philosophers did not have religious beliefs – the last quarter of Hobbes' *Leviathan* is on the Kingdom of Darkness, a consideration of the depths of his religious understanding. Burke valued religion as a potent cohering source of inspiration in society. Gerrard Winstanley was a deeply spiritual man – but he was, of course, against the established society. Rousseau had a strong sense of the mysteriousness of life. But by and large modern political philosophy is about the materialistic social and economic structure, and not at all about the numinous, the mystery of life and our relationship to the cosmos. This is very different from most societies that have ever existed, which have perceived a coherence between the stories they told themselves about the nature of the Universe and the development of the social world they were constructing in the everyday life they experienced around them, based on the more universal values they lived by.

This perception of the limitation of political and social thinking in the West is fundamental to Berlin's approach in his work. His study is of philosophers who have fought against the current, and the narrowness of modern political thought, with its restricted and secular view of human nature. As Hausheer writes in his Introduction, "the inadequacy of the simple reductionist frameworks is most keenly felt in that vast, amorphous, volatile area which comprises spiritual, moral, aesthetic and political experience.....in examining the ideas of philosophers, thinkers, men of vision like Vico, Hamann and Herder, Herzen and Sorel, Berlin displays a uniquely perceptive sensitivity to the deeper stirrings and movements, the dark, uneasy, brooding seasons of the human spirit beneath the bland rationalistic surface of the thought of an age....": they "point towards a larger and more generous (and perhaps more truthful) conception of what men are and can be." Once again, we are brought back to the query of who we are, what is our nature as human beings? And how can we in the twentyfirst century enlarge, theoretically and then practically, our assumptions of who we are spiritually and what our political world could be?

v.   The final characteristic I would like to comment on in relation to the political philosophy we are living out today is that it is completely adult on the whole, and not usually self-reflexive, self-aware. It is interesting that most of the classic political philosophers – like most children anyway in the West – had harsh or over disciplined childhoods. Most write of their philosophies as though they were only an adult product – as in one sense they are of course, because we mostly ignore the child. The child for much of this period was not seen as fully human or to be considered. But one thing we have learned in the twentieth century is that much of the way the individual tends to see things is unconsciously determined, and much is rooted in childhood. If we begin to look at the interaction between the philosopher and their philosophies, we may see more about how they were constructed and why. The harshness of the picture of the world they draw is arguably a product of the harshness of their own lives. Rousseau was more aware of this than any; he published his *Confessions* alongside his philosophy, knowing there was a connection – just as Jung's *Memories, Dreams, Reflections* is a commentary on his work. Could we from this point in human history approach political philosophy with more self-knowledge, more awareness of inner and outer worlds, more imaginatively?

The main body of Part Two then, is to consider what has been missed out and give these areas more consideration. There are chapters on the Feminine, on Indigenous and non-Western knowledge, on humans as one species among many in the natural world, on the possibility of spirit, the sacred and the numinous in the universe, and on philosophy written with self-knowledge. In this I am writing of the Other – that not presently considered. Eastern thought is far more ready to consider the other, the opposite, the both/and rather than the either/or, and it is in this way that I want to reflect on political thought in Part Three.

References

1. Roger Hausheer. Introduction to *Against the Current.* By Isaiah Berlin Pimlico. 1997 pxxiii
2. Op.cit. pxiv

Part Two

Other voices and images, largely omitted from political theory

Chapter Eight

The Mysterious Female

The Valley Spirit never dies.
It is called the Mysterious Female.
And the doorway of the Mysterious Female
Is the base from which Heaven and Earth spring.
It is there within us all the time.
Draw on it as you will, it never runs dry.

Lao Tzu

It is extraordinary how women and the whole female element have been missing in Western political thought. The *Tao Te Ching* above, an ancient Chinese philosophy, sees the spiritual female quality as the basis of creation. The earth, through many centuries of human existence, was perceived as female – Mother Earth: she was human food, shelter, support, sustenance: she was often seen as the divine in human form. This is argued most persuasively by Riane Eisler in *The Chalice and the Blade*, who begins her book not just with early history but with prehistory, gathering her evidence from artefacts not writing. She traces back to matriarchal societies, which tended to be harmonious, far less warlike, than the modern world. She looks back to the old legends of East and West – "the Bible tells of a garden where woman and man lived in harmony with each other and with nature – before a male god decreed that woman henceforth be subservient to man. The Chinese *Tao te Ching* describes a time when the yin, or feminine principle, was not yet ruled by the male principle, or yang, a time when the wisdom of the mother was still honoured and followed by all."[1]

In Taoist thought, Yin and Yang form a harmony of opposites. Both qualities are needed in any creative activity. These qualities are complementary and cooperative in creation, but they can also be mutually destructive – the existence of each is only fully possible without the other, but this is not without danger. The concept of Yang and of Yin is not just about male and female. Yang is about Light, Activity, Creation, Positive energy, Intellect, Sun, Height, Breathing out, Dynamism, Attraction, Existence, Objectivity, Spirit. Yin's energy is in Darkness, Passivity, Negative energy, Emotion, Moon, Breadth, Breathing in, static energy, Repulsion, Subjectivity, Body, Receptivity. A perfect harmony of yin and yang would be unchanging. Change comes from a growing imbalance in the system when some factors alter – environmentally in nature, socially and environmentally in human society. The universe including the earth is ever changing, so elements are altering all the time. Our world is not static.

Riane Eisler's highly respected study of the change from matriarchy to patriarchy in human history, is supported by the archaeologist Maria Gimbutas in particular where she describes the civilisation of Old Europe as depicted by archaeological evidence, and this change is substantiated by many other well-known writers acknowledged in Eisler's Introduction. These studies give evidence for an early picture of relatively harmonious societies, where 'yin' values prevailed. This did not mean that women dominated men, but that they lived in relative equality though with different roles. This is what calls Eisler calls a Chalice society. It is traceable in particular in Neolithic societies, and all societies where the Goddess is revered. In particular, Eisler writes on the Minoan society in Crete, some of the evidences of which have endured to this day.

In this story, the Chalice changed with the beginning of agriculture and with possession, with the ownership of goods and the taming of animals for food, to the societies she designates as the Blade. About 6,500 years ago, the 5th century B.C.E. – very recently in the history of the human race – these relatively peaceful societies were invaded by itinerant bands who brought with them a very different culture., coming in three main waves – around 4200 B.C.E., then 3200 B.C.E., then 2800. These were Indo-European or Aryan who brought male Gods of war and of mountains and valour. Also of course, the Semitic peoples spread with their male God Jehovah. These Gods had what Eisler calls a Dominator model of social organisation. Engels in the nineteenth century was one of the first to link the emergence of these hierarchies and social stratification based on private property with male domination over women. This is also linked by both Engels and Gimbutas with the growing use of metals, particularly for technology and weapons of war.

Riane Eisler comments that "at the core of the invaders' system was the placing of higher value on the power that takes, rather then gives, life"[2]: on death and possession rather than life. She writes that the institution of slavery, and the organised slaughter of other human beings, was legitimised here. There is archaeological evidence of spoils of war being not only animals and possessions but also women of another race or culture: women and foreign men could become possessions. These possessions can be found in the graves of important men, the people killed to die with their master.

A masculine approach is familiar to us in the basic political theories of Part One of this book. From Machiavelli onwards, men are seen as warlike and women are ignored. This is not only so for actual men and women in relation to power, but also for the qualities and powers seen as feminine and essentially subversive of male superiority. Where could the root of this skewed relationship lie? Could it be in a man's instinctive and learned fear of women? Every man was once a baby: he was cared for intimately at the most youngest and vulnerable time of his life and for years had the experience of being dependent on a woman, usually his mother: the earth herself is infinitely stronger than every man-made empire: and women have the ability to bear children, a facility necessary for the continuation of the species. But the nature of this whole quality of emotional experience is relegated to private life and conventionally seen as irrelevant to the public arena including political thought in the modern and much of Western ancient civilisations. It is lurking there as 'the other'. As D.H.Lawrence, with his customary astuteness commented: "unless a man believes in himself and his gods genuinely...his woman will destroy him. Woman is the nemesis of doubting man. She can't help it."

Much the same point if made by Hannah Pitkin in her study of Machiavelli, the first modern philosopher. In Chapter 2. She writes, "the seemingly exclusive masculine world of Machiavelli's political writings, where men contend in the arena of history, is actually dominated or at least continually threatened from behind the scenes by dimly perceived, haunting feminine figures of over whelming power. The contest among the men turns out to be, in crucial ways, their shared struggles against that power. The feminine constitutes 'the other' for Machiavelli, opposed to manhood and autonomy in all their senses: to maleness, to adulthood, to humanness and to politics.....As a counterpart to *virtu*, no epithet is more frequent or more powerful in Machiavelli's vocabulary of abuse than 'effeminate' ". Machiavelli wrote many novels and Pitkin comments on the material in these writings, "at the same time as they are contemptible, foolish and weak, women somehow possess mysterious and dangerous powers; they constitute a threat to men, both politically and personally."[3]

Politics is seen by Renaissance writers onwards as a man's game, not a woman's. And the same could apply to Hobbes, Locke, Burke, Rousseau, Marx and most of the political writing in Europe up to the nineteenth century. Even Rawls in the twentieth century does not discuss women.

Women occasionally spoke out in Europe during the earlier years when formal politics was being formed. There were also strong women leaders, such as Joan of Arc in France in the Fourteenth century and Elizabeth I of England in the Sixteenth, both assuring their followers that they had strong enough male attributes to lead.

But the most articulate protests by women were made in Europe at the time of the two political revolutions, when taken-for-granted values were openly challenged - the first revolution the Civil War in England between the King and Parliament in 1642-8, and the second at the French Revolution of 1789. At such times those ignored by the generally accepted power structure could find some opportunities to voice their discontent. There were many strong and telling protests from the powerless poor and from women in seventeenth century England when the commonwealth was created at the end of the Civil War in 1648, when power was being questioned.

Some protests by voteless men have been mentioned in the first part of this book in Chapter 4. Here also is one example of a public protest by Quaker women whose husbands had been imprisoned in the Tower of London to Parliament, and who were themselves threatened, led by Elizabeth Lilburne, entitled *A petition of women, affectors and approvers of the Petition of September 11th 1648*. They wrote, "that since we are assured of our creation in the image of God, and of an interest in Christ equal to men, as also of a proportional share of the freedoms of this Commonwealth, we cannot but wonder and grieve that we should appear so despicable in your eyes as to be thought unworthy to petition or represent our grievances at this honourable house. Have we not an equal interest with the men of this nation in those liberties and securities contained in the Petition of Right, and the other good laws of this land? Are any of our lives, liberties and goods to be taken from us more than from men, but by due process of law and conviction of twelve sworn men of the neighbourhood?...Would you have us keep at home in our houses, when men of such faithfulness and integrity as the four prisoners, our Friends in the Tower, are fetched out of their beds and forces out of their houses by soldiers, to the affrighting and undoing of themselves, their wives, children and families?...."[4]

Their efforts were not however successful. Neither women nor many men were ultimately politically liberated by the Commonwealth of 1648-60, for all its brave intentions, and for the next hundred years only the occasional woman was able to protest in any public way against their absence from the political system. Even Rousseau, who was so ready to fight for those in chains, argued that the education of men and women should be entirely different because, as Genevieve Lloyd expresses it, he thought that "the feminine was construed as an immature stage of consciousness, left behind by advancing Reason."[5]

The second opportunity for political protest about the neglect of women in the formal practice of government was at the time of the French Revolution which of course disrupted the status quo in Europe and the growing United States of America. There was one vivid protest in England that was both personal and political in Mary Wollstonecraft's *Vindication of the Rights of Women* in 1792, and this has been discussed in Chapter Six. In France itself, writers such as Condorcet and Olympe de Gouges wrote several books calling for the emancipation of women, and militant feminist newspapers demanded attention to the status of women in society: "we are suffering more than the men, who with their declaration of rights leave us in a state of inferiority, or, to tell the truth, of the slavery in which they have kept us for so long."[6] Thomas Paine in his *Occasional letter to the Opposite Sex* of 1775 supported such views in England, France and America, where he was very influential: he wrote, "even in countries where they may be esteemed the most happy, (women are) constrained in their desires in the disposal of their goods; robbed of freedom and will by the laws; slaves of opinion which rule them with absolute sway..." and he joined his protest about the Rights of Men with those of women.

Then into the nineteenth century, both women's and occasionally men's voices were increasingly heard in writing to protest against their exclusion from power. American women were particularly articulate in their call for rights under the American Constitution.

The lack of the feminine quality in politics, the yin, is not exactly the same as the rights of women, though obviously they are linked through political attitudes and values over the last few hundred years in the West. It perhaps takes the suffrage movement of the twentieth century in the shape of Christabel Pankhurst to link together women themselves with the values of receptivity, community, peace and creativity which are part of the potential 'yin' contribution to the human world. She supported the British war effort after the war had actually started, but on 7 August 1914 in the periodical *The Suffragette* she powerfully and movingly, most poignantly, wrote:

A CIVILISATION MADE BY MEN

As I write a dreadful war-cloud seems about to burst and deluge the peoples of Europe with fire, slaughter, ruin – this then is the World as men have made it, life as men have ordered it.

A man-made civilisation, hideous and cruel enough in time of peace, is to be destroyed.

A civilisation made by men only is a civilisation which defies the law of nature, which defies the law of right Government.

This great war, whether it comes now, or by some miracle is deferred till later is Nature's vengeance – is God's vengeance upon the people who held women in subjection, and by doing that have destroyed the perfect human balance. Just as when the laws governing the human body are defied we have disease, so when the law of right government is defied – the law that men and women shall cooperate in managing their affairs – we have a civilisation imperfect, unjust, savage at its best and foredoomed to destruction.

Had women been equal partners with men from the beginning, human civilisation would have been wholly different from what it is. The whole march of humanity would have been to a point other than we have reached at this moment of horrible calamity.

There are men who have a glimmering idea of something better, but only by the help of women could civilisation have been made other than cruel, predatory, destructive. Only by the help of women as citizens can the World be saved after the holocaust is ended....

Let us in everything strive unceasingly that the World may learn from the tragedy by which it is menaced, that for the sake of the human race, for the sake of the divinity that is in the human race, women must be free."[7]

This to my mind is the link. It isn't only the presence of women themselves, as persons, in the governance of society that is missing, it is a wholeness of thought and feeling within both women and men that has been unrecognised. We are governed by what William Blake called 'the ratio' - the unillumined mind, the male mind unredeemed by spirit and the feminine, perhaps changing somewhat now but for much of our fundamental political thinking over the last hundreds of years, quite absent.

The facts of male domination remain the same to the present. In the United Nations production, *The State of the World 1985,* it was pointed out that globally women are something over half the population of the world, perform two-thirds of the world's work in terms of hours, earn one tenth as much as men earn, and own one hundredth of the property that men own. Also the violence of men, the testosterone, is naturally overwhelmingly greater. Steve Jones, a well-known scientist, stated recently that the one gene that is known to be a significant factor in predicting violence, is the male one.

But there is an even more interesting aspect of the predominance of 'yang' over 'yin' in the qualities of thinking about power and the stories we tell ourselves about human nature and the kind of politics we therefore need. It is something about using more aspects of the brain and sensibility in how we see the world and make decisions about it. Fritjof Capra is very interesting in his book *Uncommon Wisdom* about the need for a wholeness in thinking which could correct the inadequacy of our present perceptions. He interviewed Adrienne Rich, an American feminist who said, "truly to liberate women means to changing thinking itself: to reintegrate what has been named the unconscious, the subjective, the emotional with the structural, the rational, the intellectual." This would mean correcting a bias that has been present throughout Western history.

That this bias has been there throughout Western political thought is the contention of Genevieve Lloyd's study *The Man of Reason: 'male' and 'female' in Western Philosophy*. She argues that from the Greek philosophers onwards, Reason was seen not as human, but as male. Reason was known as rational and about objectivity and also about the attempt to transcend nature - which was associated with the female. As Genevieve Lloyd writes, "from the beginnings of political thought, femaleness was associated with what Reason supposedly left behind – the dark powers of the earth goddesses, immersion in unknown forces associated with mysterious female powers."[8] It was the difference, in Pythagorean thought, between Form and Formlessness.

As political philosophies were created at the beginning of the modern period, the earlier philosophers, Machiavelli, Hobbes and the Renaissance thinkers, commented quite directly on the sexual nature of their writing. Francis Bacon was particularly frank. As Lloyd puts it, in his theories "Bacon united matter and form – Nature as female and Nature as knowable. Knowable Nature is presented as female, and the task of science is the exercise of the right kind of male domination over her." In Bacon's amazingly titled book *The Masculine Birth of Time*, in his view the offspring will be 'a blessed race of Heroes or Supermen who will overcome the immeasurable helplessness and poverty of the human race' and be able to dominate Matter or Nature as though she were a woman. The inequality of this relationship was consistent with the Christian teaching of the time and to this day, both Catholic and Protestant, where only men were priests and women could be seen as temptresses or, at the best, helpmates to their men.

A most powerful and telling study on attitudes of male scientists to women at the early scientific period, is Carolyn Merchant's *The Death of Nature*. She makes most vivid the sexual imagery of the Renaissance, and seventeenth century metaphors. A direct correlation was perceived between mining the earth and "digging into the nooks and crannies of a woman's body"[9] – and mining became more and more acceptable. In the pastoral imagery that became popular in the sixteenth and seventeenth centuries with Spenser's imagery and Cranach's paintings, the female was essentially seen as passive and subordinate, and ready to be exploited – just like the earth.

In more recent centuries, it has been the growth of much more independent and articulate women occurring regularly, not just oddly, in society, which gives clues to the possible development of male and female characteristics within the individual leading to a more androgynous mindset. Frances Wright, an original and independent woman of mid-nineteenth century America, expressed the leap just beginning to be made in modern times. She wrote to her friend Marquis de Lafayette in 1822, "I dare say you marvel sometimes at my independent way of walking through the world, just as it nature had made me your sex instead of poor Eve's. Trust me, my beloved friend, the mind has no sex but what habit and education give to it and I who was thrown into the world like a wreck upon the waters have learned as well to struggle with the elements as any male child of Adam."[10]

Along with this physical independence there has been a strong movement in depth psychology as well as in political thinking, towards a more holistic view of the mind. June Singer, in her book on androgyny acknowledges once again the present predominant mode of thinking: "the tradition of Western thought is primarily linear and analytical.... And so we...drive wedges between the black and the white, between consciousness and the unconscious, between the masculine principle and the feminine principle." She speaks of "the tendency of Western thought to separate out, dissect, examine and reassemble."[11] Singer argues strongly that the stories we tell ourselves based on entirely male thinking are fantasies, no more, because they miss large parts of the truth. These accords with a statement of Fritjof Capra in *The Tao of Physics:* "a fully realised human being is one, who, in the words of the Lao Tzu, 'knows the masculine but keeps to the feminine'."[12] There has been a strong body of thought in recent decades which has accepted that there are both yin and yang elements in the makeup of every person, female or male.

This has been supported by influential Jungian theories about the presence of the animus in the women and of the anima in the man – the inner realisation of the opposite polarity, and how the opposite elements are often suppressed by convention. The acceptance of the internal opposite within the person is leading to a different picture of the potential wholeness of the individual developed through life, as well as to a re-examination of social and political thought and understanding. Elizabeth Blackwell, one of the first women who trained to be a doctor in England well over a hundred years ago, pointed out in 1889, "it is not the custom to realise the positive fact, that methods and conclusions formed by one half of the human race only, must necessarily require revision as the other half of humanity rises into conscious responsibility".

George Eliot in *Daniel Deronda* spoke of her heroine Gwendolyn as "a soul burning with a sense of what the universe is not". It is surely not the universe that is at fault, but our skewed perception of it, the unsatisfactory and destructive stories we tell ourselves.

References

1. Eisler, Riane: *The Chalice and the Blade*. Harper and Row 1988 pxv
2. Eisler op.cit.p48
3. Pitkin, Hanna Fenichel: *Fortune is a Woman: Gender and Politics in the Thought of Niccolo Machiavelli*. University of California. 1984. Pp109-110
4. Hampton, Christopher: *A Radical Reader*. Penguin 1984 pp214-5
5. Lloyd, Genevieve: *The Man of Reason: 'Male' and 'Female' in Western Philosophy*. Methuen. 1984.p58
6. Rendall, Jane: *The Origins of Modern Feminism: Women in Britain, France and the United States 1780-1860*. Macmillan. 1983. p46
7. Hampton, Christopher op.cit. pp.601/2. Also see Angela K.Smith: *The Pankhursts and the First World War Propaganda. Womens History Review:12:1:pp103-118*
8. Lloyd, Genevieve op.cit. p2
9. Merchant, Carolyn: *The Death of Nature*. Wildwood House, London. 1982. p39
10. Taylor, Anne: *Visions of Harmony: a study in nineteenth century millenarianism*. Clarendon Press. 1987pp101-2
11. Singer, June: *Androgen: towards a new theory of sexuality*. RKP.1977. p38
12. Capra, Fritjof: *The Tao of Physics*. Fontana. 1979 p151.

Chapter Nine

Indigenous Wisdom and Modern Political Philosophy

I cannot bring you home again
until you hear the secret words
of silence in the air
creation that lived there
long long before the time
when time began
magic legend time
land legend spirit God
creation glowing with the
land aglow
and rain and snow
the flight of birds......

until you hear the singing trees
the crooning earth
the living dreams
until you hear
the throb of blood
inside a stone
I cannot bring you home

Kevin Gilbert: *Until You Learn* [1]

* * *

A question on the 1907 Examination question of the London
School of Economics, set by Westermarck and Rivers, well-known

anthropologists of the time: "Give facts illustrating the savage's idea of personality, and consider how far this differs from the fully developed concept".

* * *

The beautiful poem above was written by an Australian Aboriginal man in the late twentieth century and seems far removed from the political philosophy we considered in Part One: indeed, it truly *is* significantly different in many ways. The examination question below it, on the other hand, was presumably politically acceptable to prestigious universities training professional anthropologists at the beginning of the twentieth century, even if utterly unacceptable to the peoples seen as 'savages'. Indigenous myths and stories, the cultures and politics of their societies, the articulate indigenous voices, are now just beginning to be heard clearly in the modern world. One hundred years ago and before, they would have been ignored completely by political thinkers as irrelevant to the conduct or vision of contemporary society. Now at last we can begin learn from the wisdom of non-Western cultures, and consider how this could be incorporated in an extended political vision for the future.

Myths of the indigenous peoples are about their place on earth, their relationship with the universe and with death, their survival, and their search for meaning. As Karen Armstrong writes in her little book on Myth, "from the very earliest times, we have experienced our world as profoundly mysterious; it holds us in an attitude of awe and wonder, which is the essence of worship"[2] – though this is a reaction many Westerners have most regrettably lost or repressed. Of course, the early peoples were also necessarily preoccupied with survival in what was likely to be a harsh climatic world, filled with predators and disease, and possibly other hostile human cultures. In most cultures that survived for any time, there would be an overarching story to make some sense of the contradictions on all levels – some narratives harsh and warlike and others more benign. These would include all the Creation Myths.

Such over-arching cosmic stories are on a different level of enquiry from the search for order and control in a troublesome and enormously more populated world just 500 years ago when political philosophy developed in modern society, the subject of Part One of the book. The political level is based in a fundamentally different part of the human brain – a more rational, technological and scientific search is assumed to be required to develop a framework for political action. The primary human search is for meaning and Cosmos, the second for a workable Polis – a political system that meets the needs of the society. However, contrarily, in the modern world we tend to relate to the political, social level, Polis, in our search for meaning, and look to the cosmos with scientific rather than wondering eyes. This means there is little if any relationship between the communal political philosophy and politics of our time, and our understanding of the universe which now is conventionally seen in technological and scientific, not Cosmic, terms. The revised framework creates a huge gap, a hiatus, in Western society's vision, making it quite unlike the stories of the indigenous peoples of the past: it tends to leave us feeling dissatisfied and restless because many of our hopes and loves are pitched at too pragmatic a level. Politics and power itself is seen as instrumental and is not held within a wider vision: by contrast the stories of older cultures do not have a separate political theory seen as rational since power in these societies is understood within a vision of the whole of life.

This disjunction and fragmentation in Western cultural understanding is brilliantly considered by the first two Parts of Richard Tarnas's recent book *Cosmos and Psyche.* He puts the issue very clearly: "Speaking very generally, what sets the modern mind apart is its fundamental tendency to assert and experience a radical separation between subject and object, a distinct division between the human self and the encompassing world. This perspective can be contrasted with what has come to be called the primal world view, characteristic of traditional indigenous cultures. The primal mind does not maintain this decisive division, does not recognise it, whereas the modern mind not only maintains it but is constituted by it."[3] The Western world tends to be secular and practical, less comprehensive, in contrast to the older worlds engaged in a search for meaning in a mysterious and powerful universe.

Also very differently, time for indigenous peoples was circular and seasonal. For Westerners especially during the last 500 years, the significance of time, perceived as linear and ever upward, is related to the idea of progress – strongly contrasted to appreciating and responding to the seasonal and more subtly changing world around them. The kind of progress the West envisages is that of the human race striving to transform what is experienced as a world not particularly friendly to mankind, on earth or in the heavens, to one that is fashioned more to the human taste through scientific knowledge and technology. It is very managerial in intent.

The earliest humans, a species known as Homo Habilis, were alive between one and a half to two million years ago and were hunter-gatherers, living in small nomadic groups. The beginnings of the Homo Sapiens era is usually dated about 220,000 years ago. Tracing from the evidence, particularly of burial rites, we can see that from the beginning, early people have needed to tell stories of themselves, their origins, and to search for the meaning of their lives and death. A key factor in early understanding is that humans are a natural part of creation. "Indigenous peoples, such as the Native Americans and Australian Aborigines, have never assumed, as we do, that Nature exists for human benefit. Instead they have believed for millennia that we humans have a profound responsibility to the

Earth as channels for the revelation of Heaven in whatever form that might take in their own culture." writes Richard Heinberg[4]. As most early groups, before the formation of cities, lived tribally, their understanding linked up a tribal cosmic story. The great expert on the myths of early humans, Mircea Eliade, underlines this truth: "the chief difference between the man of the archaic and traditional societies and the man of modern societies with their strong imprint of Judeo-Christianity lies in the fact that the former feels himself indissolubly linked with the Cosmos and the cosmic rhythms, whereas the latter insists he is connected only with History" [5]. Indeed many people today would hardly link themselves to history, as so little is History currently taught in schools.

Eliade's book, *The Myth of the Eternal Return* takes up the theme of circular seasonal time. He argues that in earlier periods, 'reality' was defined by repetition and participation in joint human activities and ceremonies: that this reality through tradition becomes more profound and deeper with repetition through generations; this valued time is more holy, more meaningful. It binds life together. Creation of the world happens all the time: it is regenerated with every new start – the beginning of the year, the birth of a new child, the beginning of a new family. At each new beginning, properly acknowledged, 'the world stands still.' And this enables the person to withstand suffering and misfortune more stoically, held into a deeper traditional rhythm.

Much of the contrast between earlier and modern social Western models was vividly brought to light in the contrasts explorers and conquerors found in their first forays into what is now America, in 1492. The extraordinary story is told in the gripping, horrifying and well-researched book *The Conquest of Paradise* by Kirkpatrick Sale. Peter Martyr, a contemporary Spaniard writing of the Indians of Cuba, compiled the accounts of men who had been there and wrote from this compilation: "it is certain, that among them, the land is held to be as common as the sun and water; and that Mine and Thine (the seeds of all mischief) have no place with them. They are content with so little, that in so large a country, they have rather superfluity than scarceness. So that (as we have said before) they seem to live in a golden world, without toil, living in open gardens, not entrenched with dikes, divided with hedges, or defended with walls. They deal truly with one another, without laws, without books, and without Judges. They take him for an evil and mischievous man who takes pleasure in doing hurt to others." [6]. Sale comments that this story, of a culture which Riane Eisler would call a 'Chalice' society, was not found at all in Western literature before this period.

But it was not a universally accepted picture – other adventurers said that the inhabitants of the land lived like 'beasts' and were savage, or stupid. And of course, most terribly and painful to read, the European newcomers set about destroying with great physical brutality – and also with the diseases they brought over for which the native inhabitants no immunity – the peoples of the land new to them, which probably numbered in the fourteenth century as many as live there now in the twentyfirst. In the half century after the arrival of the Europeans, many millions of the local indigenous people died from Western diseases, or were slaughtered. The Europeans were looking for land, Empire, and gold, not wisdom.

It would also be hard to exaggerate the effect on Western culture of these discoveries of new lands. Empires, notably the British and other European empires, were extended and enriched to an enormous degree by conquering the territories new to the West: the discovery facilitated the growth of capitalism internationally. Also, Sale maintains, it brought into American and European thought the ideas of a free commonwealth – a society without kings, hierarchies, laws, parliaments: in addition the concept of equality was introduced to many immigrants to the American continent, to join the longstanding yearning and protests about equality which had been long present to a minority of radical thinkers in Europe. And notions of social harmony and what Sale calls 'enoughness', simplicity in living, were demonstrated and eventually admired by many.

These ideas entered the realm of political thought in the eighteenth century most famously through such writers as Jean-Jacques Rousseau and his concept of the 'noble savage'. His political writings maintained that humans were originally free. He argued that the factors inimical to freedom in the impoverished unequal societies known to him in Europe were farming done on a large scale, possession and 'civilisation'. He was particularly opposed to possession. He wrote in his famous prize essay *Discourse on the Origin and Foundations of Inequality among Men:* "the first man who, having enclosed a piece of ground, took it into his head to say 'this is mine', and found people simple enough to believe him, was the real founder of civil society. From how many crimes, wars, murders, from how many horrors and misfortunes might not any one have saved mankind, by pulling up the stakes, or filling the ditch, and crying to his fellows; 'beware of listening to this impostor; you are undone if you once forget that the fruits of the earth belong to us all, and the earth itself to nobody'"[7]. These radical ideas also fuelled both the French Revolution of 1789 and some aspects of the American War of Independence. They were obviously completely opposed to John Locke's political philosophy discussed in Chapter Three, the root of possessive capitalism and individualism.

As indigenous and Western societies have mixed, begun to co-habit, the power structure between them has been maintained, often enforced with great cruelty including slavery: it is known as racism, white over black, which has been part of the 'justification' of the gross inequality. In the Empires that developed mostly based in Europe and including of course the British Empire, time and changing ideas of the rights of human beings, have modified but not eradicated the grosser brutalities. This attitude has been based in two Western myths, two stories, one based in the belief that Rationality and Science are a superior form of knowledge and truth, and other in the myth of Progress mentioned before, backed up by the interpretation of Darwin's work as natural Evolution where the 'fittest' (Thomas Huxley's word) survive. Both these ideas can be discerned as political in the way they have been used over the centuries to maintain power over others. It is interesting that the sub-title of Darwin's *Origin of Species* (a great book in so many ways by a brilliant man) is *The Preservation of Favoured Races in the Struggle for Life.*

Bowler in his excellent study of Evolution comments that in the eighteenth century, the European was seen (in Europe) as the perfect specimen of man. "The concept of a hierarchy of races with the white man at the top had emerged long before Darwin popularised the theory of evolution. Europeans almost invariably had assumed that they were biologically superior to the races they were subjugating with their military technology....Louis Agassiz (an American anthropologist) came to believe that the black and white races were created separately as distinct forms of man, a view that could all too easily be exploited by those Americans who argued that slavery was a natural condition for an inferior race."[8] And R.H.Tawney in his classic book on the early contacts between the different cultures, *Religion and the Rise of Capitalism* comments on the mindset of an equally convinced Christian Church when he wrote that Christianity "had insisted that all men were brethren. But it did not occur to it to point out that, as a result of the new economic imperialism which was beginning to develop in the seventeenth century, the brethren of the English merchants were the Africans who he kidnapped for slavery in America, or the American Indians who he stripped of their lands, or the Indian craftsmen from whom he bought muslins and scarves at starvation prices"...because of..."the comfortable formula that for the transactions of economic life no moral principles exist."[9]

This hierarchical and secular attitude was not shared by a small minority. Alfred Wallace, for instance, who co-authored with Darwin the first paper on the theory of evolution as he had come to the same theory in the 1850s when he was working in Malaya, believed that white men could be seen as the true savages, and compared Western civilisation unfavourably with that of the people he met during his Malayan work. He wrote that "among people in a very low state of civilisation, we find some approach to such a perfect social state [in which] there are none of those wide distinctions, of education and of ignorance, of wealth and poverty, master and servant, which are the products of our own civilisation" (*The Malay Archipelago*). He also commented: "the more I see of the uncivilised people, the better I think of human nature on the whole, and the essential difference between the civilised and savage man seems to disappear" [10.] As he lived for many years in Malaysia, he could directly know what he was talking about. But there were not many who had the knowledge to think like him.

A trenchant and deep criticism of the West and the way it has proceeded in the last 500 years with the mindset described in Part One of this book, is *Barbaric Others*, published in 1993, by Zia Sardar, Ashis Nandy and Merryl Wyn Davis, a Pakistani writer, an Indian academic and a Welsh television producer living in Kuala Lumpur. This hard-hitting book describes how the West has from Greek and Roman times, all through the Middle Ages, and up to the present day, has been keen to see itself as the most civilised and most advanced group of all the nations in the world, at the van of human progress. Along with this sense of superiority has been a fear of people seen as strangers: those on the margins, those with different myths and cultures, those who do not embrace the Western science and technology and want to live differently. This reached its peak, its 'tornado' as the writers call it, in 1492 and onwards, at the sighting and occupation of the

Americas by the Spanish, Portuguese and English. They maintain that "at the epicentre of this tornado is the lie, the great lie, about the nature of the West and about the nature of the Others, about Us and Them and the relationship of all to nature: what it ought to be, what it has tragically become" [11].

This book is in fact revealing the mindset of the West from the point of view of those discounted in its equations. In my last chapter, chapter eight, we could see the critique of Western political philosophy made by women in a misogynistic system. Here in this chapter is the critique made by other cultures of the deeply racist and imperial political mindset which has pervaded much of the world through the spread of European Empires over the last 500 years.

The authors trace back the early Western and Christian Church's fear of those people living beyond the boundaries of the Roman Empire, and through to the terrors and fears of Islam in the Crusades of the Middle Ages. Those feared were seen as 'Saracens', Pagans, and savages. A Psalter map in the Middle Ages records the sort of creatures adventurers could expect to find in the Indies: with dog's heads, or with no heads but with their eyes and mouth on their torso, many performing cannibalistic acts. The authors comment on the fighting spirit of the Bible in subduing the earth and destroying the enemy, and the Greek fear of 'the barbarian' – the Cyclops, the Minotaurs, centaurs and satyrs. "The two pillars of Western civilisation, classicism and Christianity, shared a triumphalist self image" because both were intrinsic to Empires. "Each invented Otherness to define itself and the process of defining boundaries required the perennial reinvention of real peoples."[12]

We are normal and civilised, they are not. 'They' can be discounted, and the land they live on, as not occupied by 'civilised' people, can be annexed. Papal Bulls and Charters given by kings to adventurers in the fifteenth and sixteenth centuries, gave specific permission for such lands to be annexed in the name of the Christian king. The people on these lands were in general seen in a very negative light – 'heathens' and 'savages' who have none of the attributes of a country seen as normal and healthy. The Englishman Humphrey Gilbert's letters patent (11 June 1578)…empowered him to search out remote 'heathen and barbarous' lands not occupied by Christian princes. These lands could then be assumed to be empty and liable to be taken over. And it was assumed that a barbarian, if captured, could be treated as a 'natural slave'. This made the white man a 'natural master'.

The writers of *Barbaric Others* comment, "thus did the Europeans destroy a whole way of life in the name of civilisation." They went with the spirit of Machiavelli, and anticipated the warlike philosophy of Hobbes and the justifications of Locke for the possession of land. Most of the peoples in the new continent had had no concept of the ownership of land, believing land to be a free as sunshine and rain. The writers of the book maintain that 'the other' was invented out of Europe's own inner demons and fears.

This whole history of the human race, involving constant bloody war against strangers and people seen as inferior and aliens, arising from the mindsets and the myths described above, is no longer feasible as it has been lived out politically or morally in a global world. There are now interesting books by authors previously seen as 'other' working towards a different vision, and different myths. For instance, people from indigenous cultures are now becoming academics and questioning the kind of knowledge produced by Western societies. Alternative histories are being produced – a history of South Africa is obviously different seen from a black as opposed to a white perspective: even beyond that, Afrikaans, a British and a Zulu history could all read as radically unconnected to each other. And how is it at all possible to hold these unconnected truths, to enable a world of different realities to live together?

Inevitably the techniques of acquiring knowledge raise fundamental questions of meaning. A very thoughtful book, *Decolonising Methodologies: research and indigenous peoples* by Linda Tuhiwai Smith[13], a New Zealander and a Maori, argues that knowledge itself has been colonised by Western writers through its science, its world-view and its sense of superiority. She is working towards a knowledge that is not based on 'the imperial imagination' but one that could and should incorporate a different science, a different history, a renewed way of perceiving the world. She sees this as a task which has a similarity to the feminist task of questioning the patriarchal notions which underlie our world view. The political knowledge and stories we tell have to be different, and altered by this growing input from a hugely enlarged imagination. Many people have this same sense today of a new story waiting to be born. Susannah Brindle in the Quaker Australian *James Backhouse Lecture* given in 2000, asked about the possibilities for a new vision in Australia: "could it be here – on this uniquely contrary landmass, where the earth is at its oldest, most stable and most wise, where the More-than-Human world finds its strength to endure in cooperative community rather than practices that are 'red in tooth and claw', and where its indigenous peoples have learned their ways of being from close kinship with all that breathes the breath of God – that insights for a new dawning of humanity, a new way of being human, might be found?"[14]

References
1. In Gilbert, Kevin: *Black from the Edge*. Hyland House, Australia, 1994
2. Armstrong, Karen: *A Short History of Myth*. Canongate. 2005 p20
3. Tarnas, Richard: *Cosmos and Psyche:* Viking. 2006. p16
4. Heinberg, Richard: *Memories and Visions of Paradise*. The Aquarian Press. 1990. pxxix

5. Eliade, Mercia: *The Myth of the Eternal Return:* Princeton University Press. 1974pp xiii/xiv

6. Sale, Kirkpatrick: *The Conquest of Paradise: Christopher Columbus and the Columbian Legacy.* Hodder and Stoughton. 1991. p199

7. Mason,John Hope (Editor): *The Indispensable Rousseau.* Quartet Books 1979. p59

8. Bowler,Peter: *Evolution: the History of an Idea.* University of California Press. 1984. p282

9. Tawney, R.H.: *Religion and the Rise of Capitalism.* Penguin 1984. p188

10. Clements, Harry: *Alfred Russel Wallace.* Hutchinson. 1983. p32

11. Sardar Zia, Nandy Ashis, & Wyn Davies Merryl: *Barbaric Others.* Pluto Press. 1993 p3.

12. op.cit.p38

13. Smith, Linda Tuhiwia : *Decolonising Methodologies.* Zed Books 2008

14. Brindle, Susannah: *To Learn a New Song.* Australia Yearly Meeting, Society of Friends 2000

    Also see: Kapuscinski, Rysard: *The Other.* Verso.2006

Chapter Ten

The Natural World and All Creatures

Wagtail and Baby

A baby watched a ford, whereto
A wagtail came for drinking;
A blaring bull went wading through,
The wagtail showed no shrinking.

A stallion splashed his way across,
The birdie nearly sinking;
He gave his plumes a switch and toss,
And held his own unblinking.

Next saw the baby round the spot
A mongrel slowly slinking;
The wagtail gazed, but faltered not
In dip and sip and prinking.

A perfect gentleman then neared;
The wagtail, in a winking,
With terror rose and disappeared;
The baby fell a-thinking.

Thomas Hardy (1840 -1928)

There is very little mentioned in most of the political chapters of
Part One of this book about the earth and her creatures – except
for the earth as a resource for humans. It was as though most of
the political philosophers discussed there inhabited an empty

place. The scene is urban or urbanised, the thought is rational. Locke's 'man' dug into the earth and claimed it for his possession: that is the main concern.

It is true that two of the more radical writers had a very different perception. Gerrard Winstanley in the sixteenth century and Peter Kropotkin in the nineteenth century fully realised they lived in a world in which humans were one species among many million, and saw the earth and the universe as mysterious and awe-inspiring: they were also very much in the minority in perceiving that the natural and physical world is relevant to politics. Also of course, Charles Darwin and Alfred Wallace's whole lives were spent appreciating the earth and her creatures (though of course they personally killed the thousands of animals, birds and plants they sent back to England as their specimens), but they actually wrote about their passion under the influence of Thomas Malthus's theories. Their theories of evolution have proved to be very political, very much part of the capitalist perspective, the predominant myth of our time.

Theodore Roszak, in his iconoclastic and brilliantly original book *The Voice of the Earth,* published in 1992, comments on the inconsistencies in the human attitude to society on the one hand and the natural world on the other. "The sanity that binds us to one another in society is not necessarily the sanity that bonds us companionably to the creatures with whom we share the Earth...As the prevailing reality principle would have it, nothing could be greater madness than to believe that beast and plant, mountain and river have a 'point of view.'"[1] He contrasts this modern limitation and resulting picture of reality with many much earlier viewpoints, philosophies and myths that understood that what is inside of us, our inner life, is deeply connected to the life of the universe, including of course the earth and her creatures: and our outer being is of course wholly dependent on the earth. The present culture splits all this knowledge up. The study of the universe is seen as science. The study of the human mind is psychology. The study of the social and political system is known as sociology, politics and political philosophy. The spirit is something to do with religion. But these 'subjects' are not usually intellectually or spiritually connected in modern academia – and so most political philosophy does not even mention the earth and all her creatures - the only exception of course, being the human race.

This is presently changing. Part of the change is due to fear – the fear that humans have gone far too far in using the plenteous provision of the earth, so powerfully that the earth herself is changing in response. Also the fact that humans are using up the very components – like oil, metal, wood, air quality – upon which modern society depends. And that the human population is so enormous and ever growing, increasing from 1 billion in the eighteenth century and predicted to be 9 billion by the middle of the 21st Century: we have no natural predators except ourselves, and as a result, the sustainable limits of human growth will be, or have been in some cases, exceeded.

Attitudes to Nature in Europe in the early modern period.
These changes in attitude and belief which we now consider normal in the human attitude to nature, the earth and to the universe occurred when science, like political philosophy, became instrumental, mechanical, rational, in the sixteenth to seventeenth century. This was the time of the great social turmoil commented on by Donne in his poem at the beginning of Chapter 2. Morris Berman writes in his study of this period writes that for 99% of human history, the world was enchanted and man saw himself as an integral part of it. The complete reversal of this perception in a mere 400 years or so has destroyed the continuity of human experience and the integrity of the human psyche. It has nearly wrecked the planet as well. Some of the consequences of this radically changed attitude in relation to the Earth are studied in Carolyn Merchant's extraor-

dinary study *The Death of Nature: Women, Ecology and the Scientific Revolution.*

"The world we have lost," she begins, "was organic. From the obscure origins of our species, human beings have lived in daily, immediate, organic relation with the natural order for their sustenance. In 1500, the daily interaction with nature was still structured for most Europeans, as it was for other peoples, by close-knit, co-operative, organic communities.

"Thus it is not surprising that for sixteenth-century Europeans the root metaphor binding together the self, society, and the cosmos was that of an organism. As a projection of the way people experienced daily life, organismic theory emphasised interdependence among the parts of the human body, subordination of the individual to communal purposes in family, community and the state, and vital life permeating the cosmos to the lowliest stone.

"The idea of nature as a living organism had philosophical antecedents in ancient systems of thought, variations of which formed the prevailing ideological framework of the sixteenth century. The organismic metaphor, however, was immensely flexible and adaptable to varying contexts, depending on which of the presuppositions was emphasised."[2]

This was not at all to say that Nature was seen as entirely benign in relation to the human race, but only that people felt deeply related to her. Nature could be personalised as Disorder or Nurture or both, depending on the story told. She was generally seen as female: from Greek and Roman times in the West, mining the earth was very controversial, as that was frequently seen as violating Nature's body, as though she was female. Both Cosmos and Society were perceived as hierarchical, one a template of the other: God was at the top of both systems – under him were Angels in the natural system, and Kings in the social world. More of this story is told in Arthur Lovejoy's fascinating study *The Great Chain of Being,* a myth that lasted from the time of Plato to the beginning of the eighteenth century C.E... But Nature, in Christian thought, had no power to enforce her own laws, and unity in the created world "can only be maintained by moral choices; human reason must control human lust", wrote Alain of Lillie in 1202:[3] an early example of the dominating attempt to improve on and control the human lot.

But by the sixteenth and seventeenth centuries and John Donne's poem, these old powerful stories were themselves being undermined. Societies were no longer so held together by a common understanding - in Italy, where Machiavelli produced his *The Prince,* or England where Hobbes created his version of *Leviathan,* civil wars and violence were rife. The prevailing doubt and disenchantment in society affected human respect for the natural world. "The image of nature that became important in the early modern period was that of a disorderly and chaotic realm to be subdued and controlled."[4] Nature had to be managed – and so did witches, the unmanageable and 'natural' women, who were burnt to death at that time in their thousands. Also indigenous peoples outside the Western world were pictured as savages with even more determination and seeming justification. The world was seen to be out of order. Reason in politics and in the new Science must intervene to restore the world to rights, and manage the world: restoring and maintaining order became essential in much of Europe.

In this management, as Merchant writes, "the new man of science must not think that the 'inquisition of nature is any part interdicted or forbidden'. Nature must be 'bound into service' and made a 'slave'. The 'searchers and spies of nature' are to discover her plots and secrets."[5] These quotations are directly from Francis Bacon's books, particularly *The Masculine Birth of Time.* He wrote that Nature exists in three states: "She is either free and follows her ordinary course of development as in the heavens, in the animal and vegetable creation, and in the general array of the universe; or she is driven out of her ordinary course by the perverseness, insolence and forwardness of matter and violence of impediments, as in the case of monsters; or, lastly, she is put into constraint, moulded and made new by art and the hand of man; as in things artificial."[6] Nature was seen as not good enough or as too dangerous in the first two states, so that the third course was favoured by Bacon and many more. Bacon's *New Atlantis* also dreamed of enclosures for birds and beasts where experiments could be carried out to make them differ in size and shape, in colour and activity, just as humans wanted.(7). Then at last, with this increasing control over the natural world and according to this view, Mankind could at last walk into his rightful inheritance from God. Increasingly the wagtail in Hardy's nineteenth century poem at the beginning of this chapter had good reason to dread the human race.

Other writers added to the new picture of an experimental, more mechanised and artificial universe – "the empire of man over inferior creatures" as Joseph Glanvill, another English philosopher wrote in 1668. Carolyn Merchant comments that Nature came to be seen utterly differently in the most funda-mental ways: she was changed from being known as an active teacher and parent, to becoming dismissed as a mindless, submissive body. In this way, she died or disappeared, to many human eyes in the West. Such stories and metaphors have of course been questioned ever since, this questioning has come to be particularly urgent today politically as well as morally.

The Romantic Movement

The Romantic Movement occurring in the late eighteenth century and into the nineteenth is not generally seen as political, but that is because we tend to define 'political' so narrowly. The relationship of humans to the natural world has in the end to be seen politically, as we are vividly, though often reluctantly, understanding today. Romanticism was a reaction against the rationalism which was the basis of the early political philosophies of Machiavelli, Hobbes, Locke, Burke and the eighteenth century Enlightenment: whenever things swing too far one way, the contrary impetus becomes empowered. This protest was presaged by William Blake (1757-1827), with his extraordinary vision of the deep consciousness and unconsciousness of the whole world, and his protest against the limited 'single vision' of the England he knew in the eighteenth century, initiated in his view by Locke, Newton, Hobbes and Bacon:

"I turn my eyes to the schools and universities if Europe
And there behold the loom of Locke – whose Woof rages dire,
Wash'd by the water-wheels of Newton, black the cloth
In heavy wreaths folds over every nation: cruel works
Of many wheels I view, wheels without wheels, with cogs
    tyrannnic
Moving by compulsion each other, not as those in Eden,
    which
Wheel within wheel, in freedom revolve in harmony and
    peace."

His life-times work is a massive protest against the industrial revolution, the thinking that had led to it, and the cruel results of the economic and political system which enslaved both humans and the natural world.

Isaiah Berlin in his splendid book *The Roots of Romanticism* declares that the Eighteenth Century, the Enlightenment, carried the view that all human questions can – and in the end will – be answered by human ingenuity and rationality. The main aim he argues, of human thought as understood by the rationalist is the accumulation of data upon which general propositions could be constructed, telling one what to do, how to live, what to be. This was certainly the mainspring of modern political philosophy, and this is what the Romantic movement rebelled against. Romanticism is about realising the truth within yourself: it is about the wild and unpredictable, the mysterious and weird, beauty and ugliness, feelings, intuitions. It is also about the whole, whereas rational knowledge tends to split areas into subjects: romanticism can hold the opposites as being equally true, whereas in rationality, the thinker is looking for internal consistency, control and order, dividing 'the good' from 'the bad'.

Berlin studies a number of German thinkers – Hamann, Schelling, Herder who had a strong sense of the aliveness of the earth and the universe, and of the experience of wholeness within themselves – all of which they saw as being denied in the Enlightenment. They had a powerful sense of what Jung would eventually call 'the collective unconscious' – especially the dark forces - that which we suppress and which lie behind the taken-for-granted rationality of order. We also receive these alternative messages through the nature Romanticism and critique of capitalist society of the English poets – William and Dorothy Wordsworth, Samuel Taylor Coleridge, Percy and Mary Shelley - and the American transcendentalism of Ralph Waldo Emerson and Henry Thoreau. Great poetry and great writing was produced by these people in their realisation of a deep feeling for the natural world, in which they saw themselves as an intrinsic part. Michael Colebrook and Christine Avery in their book *The Green Mantle of Romanticism* insist that this movement put nature first, before people, because the human race is part of nature – we are Nature and therefore we are dependent on the whole natural system.

Having such beliefs, Thoreau found himself an outsider when he spent some years living alone at Walden Pond in New England in order the know the earth's processes more thoroughly, studying a year's seasons scientifically and methodically. He knew very well he was isolated in his community in this passion. "It is apparent enough to me, that only one or two of my townsmen or acquaintances...feel or at least obey any strong attraction drawing them towards the forest or nature, but all almost without exception gravitate exclusively towards men or society."[8] To speak of his love for wild nature and wish to protect her, was to speak alone. Robert Kuhn McGregor, in his enlightening study of Thoreau's life, *A Wider View of Nature*, confirms the isolation of search: "he was looking at the world with eyes and mind wholly unique in the New England of his time. He alone perceived the unsurpassed importance of nature, the presence of the spirit in the forests, the ponds, the mountains, the animals and the birds he loved."[9] He was at the time reading both Oriental religious literature and the history of American Indians. "both the Hindus and the Native Americans believed explicitly in the presence of spirit in nature: that each plant, each animal was an expression of the presence of God. The Hindus especially maintained that that the entire universe was one God, Vishnu, in a multiplicity of aspects. Understanding that idea, Thoreau could bear in mind as he identified each plant that he was merely naming a part of the larger whole. As his studies intensified, he could perceive that nature behaved as one vast cycle, returning always to the same sources of spiritual renewal. The human idea of progress was a sad delusion."[10] However, Thoreau was not totally isolated as he was a lifelong pupil of Emerson and in touch with both the British Romantic movement and the life and work of John Muir in Yosemite on the west coast of America.

The twentieth century and a more political awareness of nature.

The book that awakened the world population to the dangers of modern farming, with its pesticides and widespread use of chemicals on the land, was Rachel Carson's *Silent Spring*, published in 1962 in the USA. Rachel Carson was a remarkable and courageous marine biologist, a distinguished scientist, who had already produced three books on the nature of the sea, including *On the Edge of the Sea*. She had become deeply concerned about modern farming practices, which were killing many wild creatures as well as the 'pests' they were aimed at. In a talk given at Claremont in the same year (1962), called "Of Man and the Stream of Time" she said, "Man has long talked somewhat arrogantly about the conquest of nature – now he has the power to achieve his boast. It is our misfortune – it may be our final tragedy – that this power has not been tempered with wisdom, but has been marked by irresponsibility; that there is all too little awareness that man is part of nature, and that the price of conquest may well be the destruction of man himself....instead of always imposing our will on Nature we should sometimes be quiet and listen to what she has to tell us."[11]

The main focus of *Silent Spring* was Rachel Carson's attack on the use of DDT, the most powerful pesticide ever, developed in 1939, which is capable of killing thousands of different birds at once. There had been large bird kills in the region of Cape Cod where she lived. She had advocated testing the effects of this chemical to government agencies, all without result, and decided, having already become a successful author, to publish a book to alert the public. The book took her four years to write and was meticulously researched, in the context of her own deep understanding of the complex web of life that links all creatures to each other. One chapter, 'A fable for tomorrow', forecast a future town which had no wildlife left, no birds to sing in the spring.

President Kennedy took a considerable interest in the issue, as there was an enormous backlash from pharmaceutical companies, including Monsanto. Eventually government investigations led to Government supervision of DDT and it was later banned.

Rachel Carson, who had warned about the dire effects of the chemicals in the contamination of the food chain, cancer, genetic damage, and the death of entire species, herself died of breast cancer two years after publication of the book.

In the fifty years since *Silent Spring* awareness has grown exponentially. The politics of farming, of climate change, of the human relationship with the earth has emerged for large sections of the population. A new political party in England has emerged – the Green Party, which was founded in 1973 first as the Ecological Party. Similar political parties have been founded all over the world. But most of the parties remain as minorities, and though the natural world is now on the public agenda, just as the issues of equality and race are, they remain some distance away from the mainstream. These parties also inevitably operate on the same secular level, the purely political level, which all our political parties have to; there is no call for a party which has a more holistic agenda, which sees the policies it advocates at a more than practical level. This is the factor that leads to the next chapter, that of 'Spirit' which is now nothing more than an occasional optional extra, and a very suspicious extra at that, in the political world of today.

There is however one innovation that might bridge some of this gap. This is to give some rights to the earth and to wild creatures by law, as is advocated in a book by Cormac Cullinan - Wild *Law: a manifesto for Earth Justice*. There is a World Charter for Nature, adopted by the United Nations in 1982, but Cullinan's book is advocating a legal system much more fundamental – an Earth Jurisprudence. This would involve a whole different caste of mind, one where we "once more understood that the role of humans is primarily to fit in with, and contribute to, the larger Earth system and process". The Gross National Product (GDP) growing year by year, presently a goal for every nation, would become redundant; the relationship between land and human ownership would come to be questioned; the Earth Community would come to mean the rights of all the living beings of the earth, not just the humans.

The growing awareness of the significance of the Earth has been backed by the work of many scientists. A unique and well-known scientist, James Lovelock, has developed, from his own love of nature and from his scientific meticulousness as well as creativity, the idea of the earth as Gaia, the understanding that the earth is alive, a living organism as was seen in the past, made more vivid when seeing her from the human voyage to the moon: the beautiful blue-green glowing being in the heavens. He sees her alive as trees are alive: the giant redwood tree "is undoubtedly alive, yet 99 per cent is dead. The great tree is an ancient spire of dead wood, made of lignin and cellulose by the ancestors of the thin layer of living cells that go to constitute its bark. How like the Earth..."[12]; she too is living though built by the presently dead matter which was alive in the past He adds "she is stern and tough, always keeping the world warm and comfortable for those who obey her rules, but ruthless in her destruction of those who transgress. Her unconscious goal is a planet fit for life", and if humans stand in the way of this, we will be dismissed.[13] I would see this as a fully political statement: it is certainly a powerful statement about the relative reality of power in the world, between human and universe.

The poet says the proper study of mankind is man
I say study to forget all that –
Take wider views of the universe.

Henry Thoreau's Journal. April 2 1852.

References

1.   Roszak, Theodore: *The Voice of the Earth*. Touchstone Books 1993.p13

2.   Merchant, Carolyn: *The Death of Nature;* Wildwood House 1982 pp1/2

3.   op.cit. p11

4.   op.cit. p127

5.   op.cit. p169

6.   op.cit. p170

7.   op.cit. p183

8. McGregor, Thomas Kuhn: *A Wider View of Nature: Henry Thoreau's Study of Nature.* University of Illinois Press 1997. p199
9. opcit. p202
10. op cit. p203
11. Lear, Linda: *Rachel Carson: the life of the author of Silent Spring.* Allen Press, Penguin.1997. p407
12. Lovelock, James: *The Ages of Gaia.* Oxford University Press.1988. p27
13. op.cit. p212

Relevant Books not directly quoted

Avery, Christine and Colebrook, Michael: *The Green Mantle of Romanticism.* Greenspirit Press 2008

Berlin, Isaiah: *The Roots of Romanticism.* Princeton University

Cullinan, Cormac: *Wild Law: a manifesto for earth justice.* Green Books 2003

Lovejoy, Arthur: *The Great Chain of Being:* Harvard University Press. 1978

Nesfield-Cookson, Bernard: *William Blake, Prophet of Universal Brotherhood.* Crucible 1987

Thoreau, Henry: *Walden.* Signet Books 1949

Chapter Eleven

Spirit and Politics

The same stream of life that runs through my veins night and day runs through the world and dances in rhythmic measures.

It is the same life that shoots in joy through the dust of the earth in numberless blades of grass and breaks into tumultuous waves of leaves and flowers.

It is the same life that is rocked in the ocean-cradle of birth and of death, in ebb and in flood.

Rabindranath Tagore.
Gitanjali

Tagore's intuitive realisation is that what is missing in much of the modern world, including in our politics, is a felt certainty that everything is alive, and that we ourselves and all other creatures are part of a whole being, through life, through death, and it has been ever thus. This is a level of experience we could call Cosmic. The Cosmic sense is felt within all the variations of religion, and also through much personal experience of love, wonder, beauty. The Cosmic sense can be found in some individuals, and also in some societies and groups much more strongly than in others. In the West, M.D.Chenu, in his book *Nature, Man and Society in the Twelfth Century* describes the awakening that occurred to Christians at the end of twelfth century Europe: "Precisely in the twelfth century we find ourselves in an age when, in the West, Christian people, thanks to the spread of culture and thanks even more to a sensational apostolic awakening, became collectively aware of their environment......"[1] They became much more aware of the real natural world instead of only images of it. In this creation-centred Christianity, human beings were seen as a microcosm of the macrocosm of the Universe: nature was perceived as a manifestation and creation of God. The teaching and music at Chartres Cathedral, a crowning achievement created and built at that time, was based on this theme: "between 1145 and 1153, Bernard Sylvester composed his tribute to Nature, the *De Mundi Universita*te, the two parts of which set forth respectively a description of the universe as macrocosm and of man as microcosm."[2] It was believed at that time that science and mysticism would be able to work together, to enhance each other.

It was then, perhaps, that the spirituality of Western Christianity could be nearest to the Hindu vision of Rabindranath Tagore, the great Indian poet and writer who died only in 1941, and whose poetry heads this chapter. Some cultures are flooded with spirit, others have very little. The sense of the numinous is often dangerous, but the cultural lack of it makes for a much more desperate and depressed time such as we have at present. The Cosmic sense gives a person or a society a perspective of wholeness from which to see the social, political and personal aspects of living. As Carolly Erikson writes: "to the Middle Ages truth was defined differently. It was not wedded to temporal existence, to the world of individual variables. To a medieval man or woman the world of sensation was only part of a much vaster pattern of unchanging and immortal reality that stretched far beyond the boundaries of known time. Day-to-day experience occupied a finite place in this infinite scheme; it was only a pause between two eternities."[3] And at this time, knowledge itself was seen differently. St Bonaventure in that period saw knowledge, which he associated with light, as lying in three dimensions: the *lumen exterius,* the exterior light gives us knowledge of sense objects, and is the basis of empirical science:

the *lumen interius* gives us knowledge of rational and philosophic truths: the *lumen superius* is a vestige of God and here we find transcendence, beyond both sense and reason.

The political philosophy discussed in Part One of this book lies in the second category of *lumen interius*. In fact virtually all the knowledge presently taught in Universities can be categorised within the first two kinds – only reason and science are basically on our educational agenda. Wisdom and contemplation are not now the foundation of education in universities and schools, as they have been at times in the past, particularly when the first English colleges at Cambridge, Oxford and Durham were founded in the Middle Ages; this is an enormous lack at a time when the whole human species needs a wider contemplative framework from which to view the 21st century political situation. As Einstein said so clearly, you cannot solve problems from the same level as they occur. You need 'a wider view of the Universe' as Thoreau wrote, to perceive the issues clearly and in perspective.

The period studied by Chenu in the late Middle Ages came to an end around the end of the fifteenth century with the astronomical findings made by Copernicus and Galileo, in their realisation that the earth was not the centre of the universe, but revolved round the sun. The previous conviction that humans lived in the centre of the Universe, which was then thought to be relatively small and rather young (the earth was assumed to be about 6,000 years old as calculated from the Bible in the seventeenth century by Bishop Ussher) was gradually undermined, and a whole different story emerged from the science of the Renaissance and onwards. "In 1500 educated people in western Europe believed themselves living at the centre of a finite cosmos, at the mercy of (supernatural) forces beyond their control, and certainly continually menaced by Satan and his allies. By 1700, educated people in western Europe for the most part believed themselves to be living in an infinite universe on a tiny planet in (elliptical) orbit round the sun, no longer menaced by Satan, and confident that power over the natural world lay within their grasp."[4]

Brian Easlea goes on to write that "man in the magical world view" which could be ascribed to that held in the Middle Ages and before, "is situated at the centre of an enchanted world. He is at the centre of a cosmos threaded throughout by a world soul, of a network of sympathies and antipathies, of stellar and planetary influences, of signs conveying God's purpose...."[5] The disenchanted world, which we have basically lived in from the seventeenth century to this day, assumes, indeed often states, that the material world and the universe is dead – or, at least, not alive. Rene Descartes (1596-1650), who was a key supporter of the mechanical philosophy, "took the audacious step of declaring matter to be totally inert, completely devoid of any interesting property."[6] In fact, Descartes declares "there exist no occult forces in stones or plants, no amazing and marvellous sympathies and antipathies, in fact there exists nothing in the whole of nature which cannot be explained in terms of purely corporeal causes, totally devoid of mind and thought."[7] Descartes with Bacon, Hobbes, Locke and Newton introduced a way of seeing the world, a story, which has lasted to the present. They had enormous confidence in the new science – and the new politics - which sprang from their increasing control of what they saw as a non-living natural world, which came to include the whole universe.

It is science's contention today that it is 'value-free'. What this means, as Professor Alexander Koyre wrote in *From the Closed World to the Infinite Universe*[8] is "the discarding by scientific thought of all considerations based on value-concepts, such as perfection, harmony, meaning and aim, and finally the utter revalorization of being, the divorce of value from the world of facts". Modern science is intrinsically about quantity not quality, and aims rather impossibly to be free of values.

That the view of a non-alive universe has lasted in much philosophy and more science is given a vivid(or, more accurately, arid) airing in Bertrand Russell's stated presuppositions for his work in his book *A Free Man's Worship*, which was his secular statement about the philosophy of the mid-twentieth century. He expresses the despair of existentialism, as exemplified by Sartre and Camus, spelling out the following assumptions : "That man is the product of causes which had no prevision of the end they were achieving, that his origin, his growth, his hopes and fears, his loves and beliefs, are but the outcome of accidental collocations of atoms; that no fire, no heroism, no intensity of thought and feeling can preserve an individual life beyond the grave; that all labour of the ages, all the devotions, all the inspirations, all the noonday brightness of human genius, are destined to extinction in the vast death of the solar system, and that the temple of Man's achievement must inevitably be buried under the debris of the Universe in ruins – all these things, if not beyond dispute, are yet so nearly certain, that no philosophy that rejects them can hope to stand. Only within the scaffolding of these truths, only on the firm foundation of **unyielding despair** can the soul's habitation be safely built."[9] (my emphasis). This was the basis of the philosophy that was taught – though not quite so frankly – when I was at College in mid- 20th century.

* * *

However, it is truly amazing that there was a man living in the sixteenth century who came to many of the same conclusions about the scientific nature and extent of the universe as do many twenty-first century scientists – with the important exception that his work was intrinsically spiritual. He was alive at the same time as John Donne, lived in the years between Machiavelli and Hobbes, as he was born in 1548 and was burnt at the stake in 1600 for his temerity in publicising his deductions. These he made without even having a telescope at his disposal.[10] His name is Giordano Bruno, an Italian, at one time a monk but spending much of his life travelling Europe, teaching his findings though not finding many disciples.

Bruno's cosmology postulated an infinite universe with no centre, which is one single whole. In it, new abundance of matter is always being born. Motion is universal, with no absolute time. There are innumerable worlds, suns and planets, with planets revolving round suns. There are probably living beings in other worlds. "The universe is one because it has one single immanent principle that holds all the parts together, just as the human soul....holds together and interrelates all parts of the body. It is the soul of the universe (anima de universo): this is found in everything. Order is intrinsic to the universe, but it is not complete and perfect: it is open and cannot achieve complete perfection."[11]

By contrast to Bruno's perceptions, it is extraordinary how limited the average modern person is in considering the Universe: even those who study the vast spaces of its existence which we cannot individually imagine, often do so in a secular framework – how to "conquer" a planet, how to put more vehicles in space which become rubbish - when the space-time atmosphere which they are entering is so mind-blowing – far too enormous for our brains, imagination and comprehension. The awesome nature of the world is of course not limited to the vastness of space-time: it is in the smallest features of our own planet, the incomprehensibility of our own bodies which work without our conscious awareness much of the time in the most complex and intricate ways, in the sense of beauty, mystery and power which with conscious awareness we can feel so much of our lives. How Cosmos and Spirit can relate to each other is experienced in the sense of wholeness felt in some cultures – a wholeness which certainly doesn't seem to be experienced by the vast majority of people in the modern industrial world. There is no unified coherence in modern culture between the sense of the vastness of the billions of planets and the long unimaginable period of time in the fifteen billion of years existence of the Universe (as far as we know), and the politics of our own time – and their link with ourselves as individuals; no inner connectedness for most of us between ourselves, the ordinary events of our lives, the social structure, and our perception of spirit, universe, of 'God'.

Brian Swimme and Thomas Berry, as historians and physicists, open their remarkable book *The Universe Story* with this same sense that modern culture, for all its science, somehow misses the point. They write how vividly the story of the universe has given guidance, energy and sustenance to cultures throughout history, and go on to say, "In the modern period we are without a comprehensive story of the universe. The historians, even when articulating world history, deal not with the whole world but just with the human, as if humans were something separate from or an addendum to the story of the Earth and the universe."[12] Scientists confine themselves to the physical aspects of their work – indeed all modern science deals with quantity not with quality and meaning – and have split knowledge up into subjects and disciplines which obscure the whole. Knowledge is seen as about analysis not synthesis. "We are somehow failing in the fundamental role that we should be fulfilling – the role of enabling the earth and the entire universe to reflect on and celebrate themselves, and the deep mysteries they bear within them, in a special mode of self-awareness". Thomas Berry emphasises that the Universe is a **communion of subjects**, not a collection of objects.[13]

Their book is the universe story as we presently know it from the point of view of these most sensitive authors, with their vast and comprehensive knowledge of both physics and human history. Berry and Swimme see that the characteristics of the original creation must contain also our characteristics. In other words, if we were to look at ourselves today, as Hobbes and Machiavelli did at the beginning of their political philosophy work, we would need to go back not to an artificial 'state of nature' but to a curiosity about the universe as a whole. The answer to the question "who are we?" would then be very different, very much more testing for our comprehension and perception.

As ecology is developing, there are now other scientists who are incorporating a much wider framework for their under-standing. A recent book *Animate Earth* is a twenty-first century example of this. It is by the biologist Stephan Harding, whose first sentence is, "our world is in crisis, and, regrettably, our way of doing science in the West has inadvertently contributed to the many problems we face". He was drawn back while studying for a Ph.D., living with nature and animals, to a sense of wholeness which cannot be found in our schools and universities. He, with many other international scientists teaching at Schumacher College in south Devon, have come to believe that this sense of world soul, anima mundi, needs once again to be integrated into the very heart of Western culture, including science – and, I would say, political and social theory. Harding intersperses his theory with meditative reflections, giving a very different, more personal and contemplative feel to the knowledge he offers.

Stephan Harding has worked closely with James Lovelock in developing the concept of the earth as Gaia – the word used in classical Greece for the Earth Mother, the earthly presence of *Anima Mundi*, the world soul, "the vast and mysterious primordial intelligence that steadily gives birth to all that exists, that great nourishing subjectivity – at once both spiritual and material – that sustains all that is."[14] He ends his book looking at the political, social and economic implications of his message; the desirability of a steady state economy; an awareness of the common good both globally and locally which would include all living creatures, and the importance of practising deep ecology, which is an enhanced awareness that includes a sensitivity to the values, ethics and the integrity of all life but which is not mainstream in our present industrialised world.

How feasible is such shift in the world today? Stuart Kauffman in his book *Reinventing the Sacred* offers a statement about global beliefs in the world today, though he gives no evidence for his calculations. We are presently about 6-7 billion in population on the planet. He writes, "Around our globe, about half of us believe in a Creator God. Some billions of us believe in an Abrahamic supernatural God, and some in the ancient Hindu Gods. Wisdom traditions such as Buddhism often have no gods. About a billion of us are secular but bereft of our spirituality and reduced to being material consumers in a secular society. If we the secular hold to anything, it is to 'humanism'. But humanism in a narrow sense is too thin to nourish us as human agents in the vast universe we partially co-create. I believe we need a domain in our lives as wide as reality.....I believe we can reinvent the sacred. We can invent a global ethic, in a shared space, safe to all of us, with one view of God as the natural creativity in the universe."[15] To me, that still sounds like a rational not a spiritual enterprise and not yet the shift that is enough, though better than the deep despair that can affect many people today. As Thoreau said "most men live lives of quiet desperation" in the western world.

The Uprooted

People who complain of loneliness must have lost something,
lost some living connection with the cosmos, out of
    themselves,
lost their life-flow
like a plant whose roots are cut.
And they are crying like plants whose roots are cut.
But the presence of other people will not give them new,

rooted connection
it will only make them forget.
The thing to do is in solitude slowly and painfully put forth
new roots
Into the unknown, and take root by oneself.

D.H.Lawrence (1885-1940)

There is a movement now among scientists to reconnect scientific work with a sense of spirit, taking into account feeling and instinct as well as reason. At the experience level, this can be related to chaos and complexity theory: the understanding that the world is not 'ordered' but is for ever in movement – as Heraclitus in classical Greece perceived, everything is always changing, never still. "Things inter-relate, affect each other in a messy, complex, systemic fashion: they need diversity and variation: there is more than one possible future: there are tipping points where matters swing in a different way: control will have an effect but is likely to lead to unintended conse-quences: spontaneous natural patterns arise."[14] And chaos theory indicates that this is how things are, not only in our ordinary life but in the whole of the universe. "Although we humans tend to abhor chaos and avoid it whenever possible, nature uses chaos in remarkable ways to create new entities, shape events, and hold the Universe together."[17] These under-standings, which are old in eastern thought as well as some early western philosophy, question the story of the machine-like nature of life, and indicate there are live creative patterns active throughout the universe, at every level from the most minute to the planets. These patterns reoccur at many levels. In the Middle Ages there was the notion of correspondences that enabled people to read meaning at many levels of reality – as above, so below: "what happens to one part also happens to other parts, and hence to the system as a whole."[18]

As Laszlo argues in his book *Science and the Reenchantment of the Cosmos*, there is a deep coherence in natural systems that makes them both work and able to change: the biophysicist Mae-Wan Ho offers the delightful metaphor of a jazz-band: "the parts of the organism act like a good jazz band, where every player responds immediately and spontaneously to the improvisations of all the others." She notes that "the 'music' of the body ranges over more than seventy octaves....as long as the organism is alive, the music never ceases. It expresses the harmonies and melodies of the individual organism with a recurring rhythm and beat, and with endless variation. The organic jazz band can change key, change tempo, and even change tune, as the situation demands, spontaneously and without delay. There is a basic structure, but the real art is in the improvisation, where each and every player enjoys maximum freedom of expression while remaining perfectly in tune with all the others."[19] This feels like a universe you can feel at home in, rather than being a stranger in a dead and alien world.

That this aliveness of the whole universe is such an attractive vision does not mean it is true, but it is one that has been and is, held by many cultures and individuals throughout the ages. It is a part of the belief in a Creator God held, according to the figures given by Kauffman earlier in this chapter, by about half the population of the world; it is certainly part of Hinduism, Taoism and many indigenous cultures: it may indeed be a majority belief of the human race. It is a view about consciousness and relatedness at a deep level which includes feeling, intuition, as well as rationality – in other words, which engages both areas of our brains instead of only one and accords with the work of McGilchrist which will be expounded in the next chapter.

How does this relate to political philosophy? I would refer back to the first chapter about the stories we tell ourselves, and how much the stories we have now about the essentially warlike nature of societies and human beings are stories developed in a particular period in our history. I put forward the observation then that political philosophers like Machiavelli, Hobbes, Locke, Rousseau had to deduce from what they observed around them and what they knew of life, what was what they called 'the state of nature'. From that they then put forward a view of human nature, and from that worked towards the principles upon which power should be ordered. We can see now that this was greatly influenced by the seventeenth century pictures of the world and the beginnings of modern science, which has postulated that the earth, and indeed the universe is essentially inert matter. They also saw war as being an over-riding factor and failed to consider the caring and compassionate qualities in the human being and other animals. Also this whole long four hundred year cul-de-sac has not offered any coherent view of a relationship between the cosmos, the polis and the psyche because we have thought of the cosmos, including the earth and her creatures as 'it' and 'them' and 'other', not related to consciousness of humans who were seen to be unique in the world, superior to all the other living creatures we know.

There is a thoughtful and moving chapter in Laszlo's book by Jane Goodall, who has lived for forty five years of her life close to chimpanzees. She writes: "chimpanzees show emotions similar to those we label happiness, sadness, fear, anger and so on, and can experience mental as well as physical suffering. They also have a sense of humour.....They care for each other and are capable of true altruism. Sadly, also like us, they have a dark side: they are aggressively territorial, and may perform acts of extreme brutality and even wage a kind of primitive war." She also believes that chimpanzees can react seemingly spiritually to phenomena that move them. She writes "deep in the forest of Gombe is a spectacular waterfall. Sometimes, as chimpanzees approach, and the roar of falling water gets louder, their pace quickens, and their hair bristles with excitement. When they reach the stream they perform magnificent displays, standing upright, swaying rhythmically from foot to foot, stamping in the shallow, rushing water, picking up and hurling great rocks. Sometimes they climb up the slender vines that hang down from high above and swing out into the spray of falling water. This 'waterfall dance' may last for ten or fifteen minutes and afterward a chimpanzee may sit on a rock, his eyes following the falling water. What is it, this water? It is always coming, always going – yet always there."[20]

Could twentieth century humans once again live *sub specie aeterni*, under the light of heaven, with that same sense of wonder and awe?

References

1. Chenu, M-D: *Nature, Man and Society in the Twelfth Century*. University of Toronto Press. 1997 p.xvii
2. op.cit. p30
3. Erikson, Carolly: *The Medieval Vision*. Oxford Univ. Press 1976. p218
4. Easlea, Brian: *Witch-hunting, Magic and the New Philosophy*. Harvester Press 1980. p1
5. op.cit. p109
6. op.cit. p111
7. op.cit.p111
8. Mendoza, Ramon: *The Acentric Labyrinth: Giordano Bruno's Prelude to Contemporary Cosmology*. Element 1995 p71
9. Russell, Bertrand: *A Free Man's Worship*. Thomas Bird Mosher. Maine. 1923 pp6/7
10. Mendoza op.cit. p90
11. op.cit. pp133/5
12. Swimme, Brian & Berry, Thomas: *The Universe Story*. HarperSanFrancisco. 1992. p1.
13. op.cit. p243 and Chapter 13.
14. Harding, Stephan: *Animate Earth: Science, Intuition and Gaia*. Green Books 2006.p.40

15. Kauffman: *Reinventing the Sacred*: Perseus Books Group.2008. p xiii
16. Boulton, Jean (as Jean Bee). *Complexity, Form and Design,* in *Greenspirit,* edited by Marian Van Eyk McCain, O Books, 2010.
17. Briggs, John & Peat, David: *Seven Life Lessons of Chaos* HarperPerennial. 1999.p1
18. Laszlo: *Science and the Reenchantment of the Cosmos*. Inner traditions. Vermont. 2006. p7
19. op.cit. pp9/10
20. op.cit. p189

Other relevant Books used.

Berry Thomas: *The Great Work: our way into the future* Bell Tower. New York. 1999

De Quincey: *Radical Knowing: understanding consciousness through relationship*. Park Street Press. Vermont.2005

Chapter Twelve

The Child and The Self

As kingfishers catch fire, dragonflies draw flame;
As tumbled over rim in roundy wells
Stones ring: like each tucked string tells, each hung bell's
Bow swung finds tongue to fling out broad its name;
Each mortal thing does one thing and the same:
Deals out that being indoors each one dwells;
Selves – goes itself; *myself* it speaks and spells;
Crying *What I do is me: for that I came.*

Gerard Manley Hopkins (1844-1889)

Each political philosopher has to put forward, explicitly or implicitly, a story about human nature. What is a human person? What are his or her characteristics, drives and desires? And **therefore** what kind of society do we need? How should power be handled to enable the person and society to thrive? How can we create a society that truly serves the common good?

As I understand it, a key factor in the relationship between political philosopher and the formation of modern politics is the experience of childhood: it is my contention that much of our present political philosophy was written by men who had suffered a discontinuous, traumatised or uncertain childhood by any definition. Little is actually known about Machiavelli's childhood and personal history according to Hannah Pitkin[1] but the common experience of middleclass Italian children from the fourteenth to the sixteenth centuries was to be placed straight after birth into the care of a *balia* or wet-nurse, "generally a peasant woman living at a distance" with whom the child would stay for two years or until weaning was complete. The child became "wholly dependent for food, care and affection upon a surrogate, and its return to its own mother was to a stranger in an alien home, to a person with whom no physical or emotional ties had ever been established."[2] According to Pitkin, Machiavelli's insistence on the power of the Prince is intimately related to fear of the control of the feminine, the female, and the deduction we could legitimately make is that at the vulnerable time of his infancy he had been under the control and care of several different women. He also lived in one of the most warlike Italian states, where conflict was endemic.

Rousseau's mother Suzanne died about a week after giving birth to him, and his father was forced to leave Geneva, Jean-Jacques' birthplace, during his childhood: "despite these events he remembered his childhood as a happy time", writes his biographer, and he loved the countryside. Certainly Rousseau believed human nature to be essentially full of potential – but he and his wife inexplicably gave away all five of their children to an orphanage.[3] Thomas Hobbes was born in the year of the Armada, 1588: his mother was terrified at the possibility of invasion by the Spanish fleet and he famously wrote "my mother gave birth to twins, myself and fear". His father was a disgraced vicar who had to flee the country and Thomas was brought up by a wealthy uncle. He lived all his life in fear, particularly with the fear of human excesses which were likely to break out at any moment – indeed, realistically, had done so through much of his lifetime in the events around the Civil War.

But it was not just the specific details of the writers' childhoods, it was the European attitude to childhood itself that is in question. Infant mortality was very high up to the end of the nineteenth century, and until the parent was sure the child would live, "people could not allow themselves to be too attached to something that was regarded as a probable loss."[4] "All mine die in infancy"[5] remarked Montaigne about his children. Small children, writes Aries, were generally hardly perceived to have a personality at all; Aries calls them "these fragile, threatened creatures" who flit on the edges of their family's life: if they live, they become more important: if they die, that is only to be expected. Many, perhaps most, adults led tough, difficult and overburdened lives – especially mothers with many children - and children have often had to fight for recognition, or give up in despair.

In the seventeenth century, at the beginning of the scientific revolution and inspired by it, a whole series of pedagogic writers began to write books advising parents on the upbringing of children. Childhood, according to several writers, was 'discovered' in the seventeenth century, along with the nuclear family, and was categorised as a different stage of life; children began to have special childrens' clothing instead of being dressed as small adults as before and their upbringing was subject to far more attention especially in the middle and upper classes. Much of this was very harsh, based on theories of original sin which infants were understood to carry from birth and the need for order and obedience in warlike times.

Robert Cleaver and John Dod produced a book in 1621 called *A Godly Form of Household Government.* In it they write,

"The young child that lies in the cradle is both wayward and full of affections: and though his body is but small, yet he hath a reat (wrong-doing) heart, and is altogether inclined to evil....If this sparkle be suffered to increase, it will rage over and burn down the whole house. For we are changed and become good not by birth but by education.....Therefore parents must be wary and circumspect.....they must correct and sharply reprove their children for saying or doing ill."[6]

John Eliot in *The Harmony of the Gospels* writes later in the seventeenth century, (1678):

"the gentle rod of the mother is a very soft and gentle thing; it will break neither bone nor skin; yet by the blessing of God with it, and upon the wise application of it, it would break the bond that bindeth up corruption in the heart...withhold not correction from the child, for if thou beatest him with the rod he shall not die, thou shall beat him with the rod and deliver his soul from hell."[7]

It was thought that children would not remember beatings from that very early period, and if their wills could be broken at that time, they would not recollect afterwards that they ever had a will. The aim was for children to become obedient and to continue in obedience all their lives: they would not then be swayed by the original sin in which they were believed to have been conceived and which they brought into the world at birth. This is likely to have been the experience of children in the sixteenth through to the nineteenth, even twentieth, centuries in all classes of society. From such religious fundamentalist beliefs, is it not likely that children would be assumed to be intrinsically aggressive, needing strong control in both State and family: for this was the assumption upon which children were brought up. Hobbes particularly wrote that the order which should be imposed in the State to control unruly humanity, should be supported and indeed would be dependent on order as an essential feature of the family. He clearly saw that the upbringing of children was directly related to the politics that could be practised in any society. His view was that the relationship of child to father must be that of obedience – he wrote that the Father of the family who, in giving a home to his child, and therefore who gives "sustenance to another, whereby to strengthen him, hath received a promise of obedience in consideration thereof. For else it would be wisdom in men, to let their children perish, while they are still infants, than to live in their danger or subjection, when they are grown."[8] It is in the father's interest to tame his children, and it is in society's that he does so, as else social order would collapse.

This view of childhood and the pedagogy it involved has continued all through the period of the eighteenth, nineteenth and twentieth centuries, although with protests and alternatives particularly in the last sixty years: such alternatives have been advocated and practised in both homes and schools. This does not mean that children have not been loved, as of course they have, but that the standard ways of bringing them up, exemplified for instance by Truby King in the twentieth century, have been determined by our standardising culture. The following poignantly scenario describes a typical middle class situation not unfamiliar to most of us:

"She straightens baby's vest and covers him with an embroidered sheet and a blanket bearing his initials. She notes them with satisfaction. Nothing has been spared in perfecting the baby's room, though she and her young husband cannot yet afford all the furniture they have planned for the rest of the house. She bends to kiss the baby's silken cheek and moves towards the door as the first agonised shriek shakes his body.

Softly, she closes the door. She has declared war on him. Her will must prevail over his. Through the door she hears what sounds like someone being tortured. Her continuum (instinctive) sense recognises it as such. Nature does not make clear signals that someone is being tortured unless it is the case. **It is precisely as serious as it sounds.**"[9]

An impassioned criticism of the pedagogy advocated above has grown relatively recently with Alice Miller's *The Drama of the Gifted Child and the Search of the True Self* in 1979 and her subsequent books including *For Your Own Good: hidden cruelty in childrearing and the roots of violence* (1980). *The History of Childhood: the untold story of child abuse* by Lloyd de Mause in 1991 is a subsequent study and there are now several others. De Mause's first lines in his study sum up the argument, based on careful evidence from the past: "the history of childhood is a nightmare from which we have only recently begun to awaken......and where historians usually look to the ....battles of yesterday for the causes of those today, we instead ask how each generation of parents and children creates those issues which are later acted out in the arena of public life."[10] Indeed, it would be legitimate to argue that the root of all war lies in the lack of time and perception given to children, and the positive neglect, disruption and cruelty experienced by others. The nuclear family is a very chancy matter for children – all your eggs are in one basket: today something like a half to a third of all marriages and partnerships with children break up: most murder and abuse of children occurs within families even though such attention is given to paedophiles outside the family: and each year there are about 80,000 children in care in this country.

A remarkable book *The Continuum Concept* was published by Jean Liedloff in 1975, and I was lucky about 20 years ago to attend her seminar in London. She is quite clear that the traditional Western way of bringing up children is essentially depriving them of the fundamental safe security in the world that all humans, and indeed all mammals, need to become fully themselves. She lived for several years with the Yequana Indians and was able to observe and take part in the practice of 'holding' small children throughout their first years of life. The children constantly lived in someone's arms, night and day, until they were ready to find something of their own way – and even then the arms and comfortable body stayed available throughout their childhood. Morris Berman, who is one of the few writers who perceives that child upbringing is intrinsically connected with the social and political world - as the child is father to the man - gives examples of similar more benign practices in other societies through to modern life. "In Bali, for example, the child is carried on the hip or in a sling, in almost constant contact with the mother for the first two years of life. During the first six months it is never *not* in someone's arms except while being bathed...."[11] Some of this understanding and practices such writers encourage are thankfully coming back in the West and some families are at last changing the nature of their care and their capacity, with our present enhanced understanding of the needs of children, to actually *notice* each individual child.

A further most important difference was noticed by Liedloff which is about non-possessiveness and non-judgment of children by the adults around. "The notion of ownership of other persons is absent among the Yequana. The idea that this is 'my child' or 'your child' does not exist...the Yequana do not feel that a child's inferior strength and dependence upon them imply that they should treat him or her with less respect than an adult."[12] They are not regarded as possessions, as children often are in the nuclear family system.

The significance of these contrasting introductions to life in the general experience of children in Western society – no-one's 'fault', as the pattern is carried on down through the generations if not realised by the individual and recognised and hopefully reconsidered – is discussed further in the last section of this book, but for now I just wish to make the point that it matters greatly who a political philosopher *is*, where he or she is coming from: the political philosophy we have at present was carved out in a tough and often cruel world, for children as well as for adults. Though child rearing practices are beginning to be revised in a somewhat more benign world for many people, the very controlling methods of past centuries have been the lot of perhaps most people living today. And their echoes are deep in the controlling systems of the state, politics, and the families of busy modern society.

Through the work of Donald Winnicott and many others we have come to appreciate that newborn babies live a year to eighteen months in an entirely feeling world – "children are feelings on legs", as one very experienced mother said to me. As Liedloff writes, "The earliest established components of an infant's psycho-biological make-up are those most formative of his lifelong outlook. What he feels before he can think is a powerful determinant of what kind of things he thinks when thought becomes possible. If he feels safe, wanted and 'at home' in the midst of activity before he can think, his view of later experiences will be very distinct in character from those of a child who feels unwelcome, unstimulated by the experiences he has missed and accustomed to living in a state of want – though the later experiences of both may be identical."[13] One reads much western politics and religion, and feels it has been written in a state of depression, fear or anger.

The way we were treated as small children is the way we treat ourselves for the rest of our lives, and that is the way we are likely to treat others - though it is possible with growing self-knowledge and life experience, to change or at least modify early patterns. As Alice Miller writes, "my belief, based on my experience as an analyst (is) that human destructiveness is a reactive (and not an innate) phenomenon...."[14] Children are alright when they are born, equipped for life as is any creature. It is how they are treated and cared for afterwards, especially immediately afterwards, that matters.

How could we now see the person as the basis of a new politics?

In the twentieth century and onwards a different picture of the person, of human nature, has developed, which incorporates the width of understanding, ancient and modern, eastern and western, scientific and spiritual to which we now have such brilliant access. This picture, this story, has been known as 'depth psychology', beginning with Freud's *The Interpretation of Dreams* published neatly in 1900, and developing though to the present day. Its values are summed up to a large extent in the Perennial Philosophy, and it has in its later development in Jung and Assagioli incorporate that vital link between a person's relationship to the Universe, to society around and to him- or her -self: the cosmos, the polis and the psyche that has been mentioned earlier in this book.

Carl Jung published some thoughts on this issue in 1933 in his *Modern Man in Search of a Soul,* writing that in that dangerous period of the twentieth century between the world wars when people desperately needed to consider the nature of the human psyche: he acknowledged that "today we can no longer get along unless we give our best attention to the psyche."[15] He wrote that he was losing his faith in the possibility of the notion of an entirely rational and scientific organisation of the world, about which 'modern man' was also becoming a sceptic. His view was that it is true that "much of the evil in the world is due to the fact that man in general is hopelessly unconscious, as it is also true that with increasing insight we can combat this evil at its source in ourselves."[16] He believed that the human task was to make the unconscious conscious in ourselves as individuals and in social systems of which we are a part. We need to learn how we can grow into our own real potentiality, the quality which is at the centre of Gerard Manley Hopkins poem at the beginning of this chapter: and for this growth to be possible it is desirable for it to be fostered and nourished from birth; or if that experience has been less than benign, how to work through this in later life: but the experience of childhood is key.

Over the last hundred years an image and a story of human nature has developed which incorporates both western and eastern thought and understanding. These personal, social, spiritual and increasingly ecological and which could now be offered as a basic model for thinking about social and political systems. It is one based just as much on Eastern and indigenous values as on modern western thought, particularly insofar as it uses the yin/yang understanding that opposites are always present in the natural world, and in ourselves. It is an understanding that we are born whole, and that we seek in many ways our own potential as do all animals. Carl Jung is the best known creative force in this movement, originally building on but then splitting off from the path-forming initiative of Sigmund Freud: Roberto Assagioli developed a similar model in Italy, and this I have trained in and taught, and written a book on – *A Psychology with a Soul*.[17] Their work is on the modern personality structure, where the human feels he or she is clearly a separate individual – quite unlike some of the older cultures where the person felt almost part of the earth at times and certainly part of his tribe: where the development of the ego (the centre of the field of social consciousness) is necessary for the person to be able to maintain him- or her-self in the modern world and to achieve: and where the conscious self is contained within an unconscious which is both personal and collective: a complex personal organisation of the psyche which is required for a complex culture.

Deep within this structure is an 'I', and observer who is more, or less, present, giving an inner sense of self ('that of God' as the Quakers say) linked with the soul of the world, the anima mundi, who will also be variably present to the particular individual. As Murray Stein writes in the introduction to his study of Jung's work *Jung's map of the soul* "for him – as for us still – the human psyche is a vast territory, and in his day it had not yet been much studied. It was a mystery that challenged the adventuresome with the prospect of rich discovery and frightened the timid with the threat of insanity. For Jung the study of the soul also became a matter of grave historical importance, for, as he once said, "the whole world hangs on a thread and that thread is the human psyche."[18] The tremendous work that has been done by many writers, therapists, scientists is certainly far more profound and real than the models and stories of the person used in the basic work of political philosophy at the beginning of the modern era.

We are lucky that William Wordsworth, a Romantic poet, a man raised in the Lake District, who at the turn of the eighteenth/nineteenth centuries which was an industrial and increasingly capitalist time, presented some of this story in a poem. It is a poem that is one of the best known in the English canon, and I give here a shortened version of it.

Ode

Intimations of Immortality from Recollections of Early Childhood

There was a time when meadow ,grove, and stream,
The earth, and every common sight,
To me did seem
　　Apparelled in celestial light,
The glory and the freshness of a dream.
It is not now as it had been of yore; -
　　Turn whereso'er I may,
　　　　By night or day,
The things that I have seen I now can see no more.

The Rainbow comes and goes,
And lovely is the Rose;
　　The Moon doth with delight
Look round her when the heavens are bare;
　　Waters on a starry night
　　Are beautiful and fair;
　　The sunshine is a glorious birth;
　　And yet I know, where'er I go,
That there is passed away a glory from the earth..........

The pansy at my feet
Doth the same tale repeat:

Whither is fled the visionary gleam?
Where is it now, the glory and the dream?

Our sleep is but a sleep and a forgetting:
The Soul that rises with us, our life's Star,
        Hath had elsewhere its setting,
        And cometh from afar:
Not in entire forgetfulness,
And not in utter nakedness,
But trailing clouds of glory do we come
        From God, who is our home:
Heaven lies about us in our infancy!
Shades of the prison-house begin to close
        Upon the growing Boy,
But he beholds the light, and whence it flows,
        He sees it in his joy;
The Youth, who daily further from the east
        Must travel, still is Nature's Priest,
        And by the vision splendid
        Is on his way attended;
At length the Man perceives it die away,
And fade into the light of common day.....

        Though nothing can bring back the hour
Of splendour in the grass, of glory in the flower;
        We will grieve not, rather find
        Strength in what remains behind;
        In the primal sympathy
        Which having been must ever be;
        In the soothing thoughts that spring
        Out of human suffering;
        In the faith that looks through death,
In years that bring the philosophic mind......
Thanks to the human heart by which we live,

Thanks to its tenderness, its joys, and fears,
To me the meanest flower that blows can give
Thoughts that do often lie too deep for tears.

References

1   Pitkin, Hanna Fenichel: *Fortune is a Woman.* University of California Press. 1984. p173

2   de Mause, Lloyd: *The History of Childhood: the untold story of child abuse.* Bellew Publishing. 1991. p184

3   Hope Mason,John: *The Indispensable Rousseau:* Quartet Books 1979 p23

4   Aries, Phillippe: *Centuries of Childhood.* Penguin 1986

5   Miller, Alice: *For Your Own Good: hidden Cruelty in Child-Rearing and the Roots of Violence.* Penguin 1983. Preface.

6   op.cit

7   Jacobson, Norman: *Pride and Solace. The functions and limits of political theory* University of California Press. 1978 p82

8   Liedloff, Jean: *The Continuum Concept: in Search of Happiness Lost.* Penguin 2004. p73

9   de Mause op.cit.p1

10 Berman, Morris: *The Reenchantment of the World.* Bantam Books. 1984. p159

11 Liedloff op,cit. p97

12 Liedloff op.cit. p50

13 Miller op.cit. p142

14 Jung, Carl: *Modern Man in Search of a Soul.* RKP. 1981 p232

15 op.cit. p237

16 Hardy, Jean: *A Psychology with a Soul.* Woodgrange Press 1989

17 Stein, Murray: *Jung's Map of the Soul.* Open Court 1998. p2

Part Three

A more comprehensive view of Politics, including the Other

Chapter Thirteen

Alternative views of human nature

When Thomas Hobbes looked out at his world in the 1640s, he saw England submerged in civil war. He was born in the year of the Armada, and all his life had lived in warring and contentious situations, from his experience in his family through to living in the combative states of Europe. He, not surprisingly, came to the conclusion that 'man' is naturally warlike.

The secular picture of human nature was most famously expressed by Alexander Pope in his witty poem written a hundred years after Hobbes:-

Know then thyself, presume not God to scan;
The proper study of mankind is Man.
Plac'd on this isthmus of a middle state,
A being darkly wise, and rudely great:
With too much knowledge for the sceptic side,
With too much weakness for the stoic's pride,
He hangs between; in doubt to act, or rest;
In doubt to deem himself a god, or beast;
In doubt his mind or body to prefer;
Born but to die, and reas'ning but to err;
Alike in ignorance, his reason such,
Whether he thinks too little, or too much:
Chaos of thought and passion, all confus'd;
Still by himself, abus'd, or disabus'd;
Created half to rise, and half to fall;
Great lord of all things, yet a prey to all;
Sole judge of truth, in endless error hurl'd;
The glory, jest and riddle of the world!

Pope has so brilliantly captured the paradox, but has specifically omitted the Spirit.

George Fox and Gerrard Winstanley, looking at and living through that same 1640s in England as Thomas Hobbes, came to different conclusions yet again, accepting both paradox and contraries, and including spirit. They both acknowledged 'the river of darkness' in human nature but reckoned that darkness could be combined with a 'river of light' and that both streams, with the help of the spirit within us all, could be transformed into something greater. The deepest knowledge that we have, which Fox called the 'seed', is within us. In this view, the human world is so cruel because people in general are not enough in touch with themselves, their own nature and inner journey: they act out their own darkness in the world as individuals and as societies, externally fighting those people and elements they perceive as their enemies, because they have not come to terms with the darkness and conflicts within themselves. A world at war, within the person, in the family, in the community, in the countries, is in this view, the result of the actions and perceptions of a person or a society out of touch with that which is deepest and most whole within themselves.

The question of who we are, what is human nature, is fundamental to the kind of politics we require. A view of human nature alternative to that of Hobbes and Locke, the one which is what I would like to present here, is not a new one. Indeed it is far older, and more widespread than the 'realistic' views taken in much modern Western political philosophy. It assumes that the creation of the world did not just happen once, but that it is still going on. We as creatures of the universe share in all the varieties of opposites which exist in the universe – creation and destruction, dark and light, male and female, inner and outer, and so on – and have to learn personally and as a society to live with these contradictions in our own nature: these opposites are the source of all creativity but need self-knowledge and growing self-awareness to flourish fully within us. All birth is difficult, and the birth of the **conscious** awareness of which human beings are capable is very difficult personally and collectively. We have to work through a lot of the unconscious, driven material into which we are born, at both the individual and the collective level, and begin to see the world with clarity and inner and outer awareness. Because this process is only patchily achieved, (except in a few remarkable individuals, and perhaps in a few spiritually aware societies), then the pangs of birth are more obvious to us than the fulfilment of the potential of that same birth. It is, in my view, because in the West we generally are unaware - unaware of spirit, of the enormous significance of childhood in becoming more fully conscious, of the earth and the Cosmos, of the wisdom of older societies and of the feminine, that we find it so difficult to grow naturally into our true potential as individuals and as societies. These factors, discussed in the previous five chapters of this book, combine to make a much more complex picture of human nature - one which is the necessary basis for a new politics.

The human heart can go the lengths of God.
Dark and cold we may be, but this
Is no winter now. The frozen misery
Of century's breaks, cracks, begins to move;
The thunder is the thunder of the floes,
The thaw, the flood, the upstart Spring.
Thank God our time is now when wrong
Comes up to face us everywhere.
Never to leave us till we take
The longest stride of soul men ever took.
Affairs are now soul size,
The enterprise
Is exploration unto God
Where are you making for? It takes

So many thousand years to wake
But will you wake for pity's sake?

A Sleep of Prisoners, Christopher Fry.

It was not until well in the twentieth century that a significant number of western thinkers began to take seriously the wisdom of ancient Eastern religions, or of the peoples all over the world more consciously related to the earth than our society is. All these cultures were more stable, more unchanging, than ours. People within them are were, and are, seen as potentially in touch with a harmony in the nature of things – including the 'seed' within themselves. Helena Norberg-Hodge often comments on the level of happiness and contentment in Ladakh society which she has lived in and visited over twenty years, and which is unmatched in the West.[1]

In Hindu philosophy, the life's journey was, and is, seen in terms of stages. The first task is to become a person, growing up through learning, through trial and error, held within a network of relationships, to become the kind of man or woman required by that society. The personality has to be created first. Then the person becomes a householder, and fulfils the tasks of partnership and having children, and/or in creative and spiritual work: living in the world, enjoying it and contributing to it: this period can last for many years through the middle of life, and is one's contribution to the material and social world of humanity and the earth. However, the final two stages of life are seen as the most significant; then you may leave your earthly home and give up all your goods, in order to lose the ego, the personality, and empty yourself to allow for the soul to fully mature. There is an attitude of mind that can develop which makes no distinction between mine and thine and which can look on the whole world as one's own, or belonging to God. The intention is to link a growing recognition of the 'seed' (Atman) within oneself with its identity in Brahman, the creative spirit of the world. The antici-pation of the journey of later life affects the whole of a person's life.[2] The journey is not of course seen as an easy one, in that the person is always dealing with light and dark forces, conscious and unconscious awareness, enemies within and without, pain, suffering, death and love.

Buddhism offers a similar picture and suggests a comparable alternative to the Western view. "Like other great religions, Buddhism teaches that each of us has a True Nature, a Buddha (Awakened) Nature revealed when we become aware that mortal fear is not a necessity of the human condition."[3] Fear is created, from this view, from the existential dread of uncertainty: the driving need for security and order springs from a mortal fear about the world and the lack of safety in it, as perceived by the unawakened individual. This fear leads us to arm ourselves, defend ourselves, in all sorts of ways. Buddhism recognises the "rooted, deluded and **driven** condition of unawakened humanity."[4]

In the Buddhist view of the person, we are born into a particular individual and collective karma – that is, into the unconscious, driven material through which we have to work to find the clarity, the seed, the truly conscious state of which we are potentially capable. People are born into a particular set of circumstances, usually a family, and a particular society, which is created by human beings but which is largely seen as though it was 'the other'. There are strong irrational factors in the world which, especially with modern communications, we can see reflected in the suffering endured by living beings over the whole of the planet. Hobbes, faced with the unendurable circumstances of his own society, sought peace through the imposition of a powerful state because the sense of orderliness was flamboyantly absent in the world around him. But of course, to build up a world out of a sense of despair is to prolong the power of driven, unconscious forces.

In the Buddhist view, human beings are capable of reaching a state of clarity, of living without fear and ego by means of facing the darkness and following a spiritual (not necessarily a religious) path. This is a different state of reality from the driven one, a reality where both beauty and pain are more deeply perceived within a framework which is not defined by the narrowness of the human ego or personality. Then true compassion can move the life of that individual, and she or he can live with love and not through fear: then both understanding and action come from a different place. To the extent that the individual has travelled along this path, here is no separation between the individual and the whole world; evil is here seen as splitting, cutting off, dualism which is so much a feature of our materialistic world. Our own 'well-ordered' world, which provides material security for the few, is full of fear for all, destruction for the earth, constant wars, and allows many millions of people and animals to starve and suffer every day.

The inner perception and the world we create, the psyche and the polis, are seen as deeply related to each other in the Buddhist view. The Bodhisattva vows to come back to earth time and time again until all suffering is ended because then the newly conscious perspective will have been attained throughout all the earth.

The Buddhist comment on our ways of being in the world has a particular relevance for Western science, and for our political philosophy. "Our tendency to divide the perceived world into individual and separate things and to experience ourselves as isolated egos in this world is seen as an illusion which comes from our measuring and categorising mentality. It is called *avidya*, or ignorance, in Buddhist philosophy and is seen as the state of a disturbed mind which has to be overcome: 'when the mind is disturbed, the multiplicity of things is produced, but when the mind is quieted, the multiplicity of things disappears'."[5]

This alternative understanding of human nature is not of course found only in the East. Meister Eckhart in the European Middle Ages maintained that we only know God through knowing ourselves, and that this is a lifetime's journey. "To be a Person, then", he said, "means to have learned the secret and paradoxical art; to go out, and yet remain within; to exert power, yet exercise restraint; to transcend, and yet remain oneself; to be in movement, yet to be in total repose."[6] This is to hold the opposites, to live simultaneously in the world and in the spirit.

This ancient knowledge about the nature of people has been brought into the modern era partly because non-Western knowledge now tends to be seen with more humility by us than it was in the previous centuries when Europe was sure it was in the van of human progress. Now, understanding more clearly our destructive potential, we are not so sure of ourselves. Also this knowledge has been made directly accessible at the intimate level of therapy – particularly through the researches of Jung and Jungians, and the development of psychosynthesis[7] and other transpersonal therapies. The general Western picture of human nature, including our own, can be understood as skewed, as it emphasises the evil, weak, unworthy, unhealthy qualities: this myth is endemic not only in philosophic and religious writing and practice, but in our deepest living perception of ourselves. To realise that the old hard personal issues can be worked with, softened and transformed, that our individual and social troubles can be seen in an infinitely wiser, larger and more dynamic framework is not only an intellectual revelation, but also an emotional and spiritual one for the many who discover depth psychology or find the path of what Jung calls 'individuation' by other means.

Individuation is what Jung calls his picture of the soul's journey. He believed this journey often begins when the person-ality is wounded: the accommodation that has been made through an individual's life until then, to cope with the wounds, the unresolved issues and the unconscious forces common to us all, is broken. Then the true life's journey, the equivalent of the third and fourth stages of the Hindu tradition, can begin. The process of individuation is one of relating to and integrating all the parts of oneself, even those most hidden: it is naming and recognising the major paradoxes of one's nature, and beginning to see from a clear centre. This releases love and energy, and begins to make space for the spirit.

The collective process is the same as the individual one: all that is presently repressed and ignored, despised, on earth, can be seen and named. This is perhaps what we doing now with our greater painful acknowledgment of the terrible things happening in the world – the way we are destroying the planet, the way that we seriously illtreat other species, sometimes to extinction, the wars, the starvation, the massive armaments treated purely as commercial products – no morality involved – the child abuse and the genocide. It is not until we name the horrors and fears on the personal or the collective level that we can begin to work to transform them. The immediate communication through mass media make them infinitely more obvious than they have been before in history. But of course what we define as problems depends on the level of compassion within the way we see things. The more open to beauty and the spirit we are, the more we are able to acknowledge our own and others' suffering.

Teilhard de Chardin spells this out in passages in *The Divine Milieu*. "It is we, who, through our activity, must industriously assemble the widely scattered elements. The labour of seaweed as it concentrates in its tissues the substances scattered, in infinitesimal quantities throughout the vast layers of the ocean; the industry of bees as they make honey from the juices broadcast in so many flowers – these are but the pale images of the working-over that all the forces of the universe undergo in us in order to reach this level of spirit" …. The human being helps to make his own soul "through his earthly days; and at the same time he collaborates in another work, in another opus, which infinitely transcends, while at the same time narrowly determines, the perspective of his individual achievements: the completing of the world."[8]

This view postulates that we and the world around us are of the same stuff, in every way. As Avens comments, "contrary to the dominant Western view extending from Plato and Aristotle to Averroes and Aquinas and culminating in Descartes, the knower is not divorced from the known, the inner from the outer, the self from the world. We are enabled to know the so-called outside world only because something of that outside world (anima mundi) is also inside ourselves. In theological language this would imply that God (or cosmos) is knowable, but we cannot know him until we become similar to him."[9]

The promise of an emergence of true human nature is essentially related to the level of consciousness. Whilst people are driven, by power, by goods, by material possessions and by the need to possess others, they will **inevitably** live destructively and inappropriately in relation to the greater whole, and have to exert control by draconian means – the sort of control that is the subject of much political philosophy and state power. If we could learn to live 'in the spirit' there would be no need for artificial constraints because the right action would be more obvious. Then you can truly live not causing suffering, not casting your shadow.

A nursery rhyme.

There was a little girl, and she had a little curl,
Right in the middle of her forehead.
When she was good, she was very, very good
But when she was bad, she was horrid.

Jung was very clear the myth, image, of human nature being discussed here involves a search not for goodness ('very, very good' as the above rhyme says) but for wholeness. We become twisted and onesided trying to be "good", as children are exhorted to be. Being good in society means suppressing the evil; but evil suppressed will inevitably emerge somewhere else. "Whenever prolonged onesidedness occurs within the conscious attitude of the individual, a countering compensatory action takes place within the unconscious....the stone rejected by the builder becomes the cornerstone of the prisonhouse, in which the builder comes to be confined. As with the individual, so with the culture; onesidedness breeds insanity. The excessive conscious-pursuits of rational values bring unprecedented outbursts of irrationality; rigid insistence on consciously accepted ethical maxims occasions the rise of crime and violence; and the perpetually avowed pursuit of world peace leads to the outbreak of one horrendous world war after another."[10] While not fully agreeing with the last statement, I do see that you cannot just suppress the bad, the evil: you have to face it and live through it. It is only by doing this that the opposites become reconciled and there is a possibility of wholeness.

Once the journey to wholeness is being sought and hopefully lived out to some extent, then there can be an identification with the whole world. The person who can feel and act with compassion for all living creatures we tend to see as a saint – but perhaps they are feeling what we were all born to feel and live out, coming trailing our 'clouds of glory', before the prison house begins to close upon us with our socialisation into society. Jung said: "at times I feel as if I am spread out over the landscape and inside things, and am myself living in every tree, in the plashing of waves, in the clouds and the animals that come and go, in the procession of the seasons."[11] This reminds one of the seventeenth century mystic Thomas Traherne: "you never enjoy the world aright till the sea floweth in your veins, till you are clothed with the heavens and crowned with the stars."[12]

The contrast of this view of the potentiality of people compared with the assumption that 'men' (at least) are intrinsically warlike, will seem impossibly optimistic to some. Looking at the world today, we see the horrors. It seems more 'realistic' (a favourite conservative word) to see human nature as inextricably flawed, possessive, competitive, aggressive, not to be trusted. But what if those views are a self-fulfilling prophecy? Because we underestimate ourselves, we erect great barriers to our own potential, both within the personality and in political and economic structures. Abraham Maslow started his work by studying people not from the point of view of problems, but by considering those who seem most successful and most fulfilled in the world. He maintained that in mid twentieth century America, "the normal adjustment of the average, commonsense, well adjusted man implies a continued successful rejection of much of the depths of human nature.....To adjust well to the world of reality means a splitting of the person. It means the person turns his back on much in himself because it is too dangerous. But it is clear that, by so doing, he loses a great deal too, for these depths are also the source of all his joys, his ability to play, to love, to laugh, and, most important for us, to be creative. By protecting himself from the hell within, he also cuts himself off from the heaven within."[13] If virtually all our influential political philosophies, as I maintain they are, are built on a view of human nature that is depressed and repressive, then it is no wonder that we are not living at ease with ourselves and with all the creatures in the world. And if we don't look beyond the material and into the spiritual, then we cut ourselves off from our highest potential, and a sense of perspective that could enable us to perceive human problems from a wider framework.

Most of the philosophies we have touched on so far imply that most people in the West live their lives half asleep, unconsciously. The obedience and authoritarianism we learn very young demand this; the lack of spiritual awareness in our society offers little else; and in a highly unequal world, many groups are too poor to aspire to much hope, and others too powerful and dominant to be prepared to drop any defences. The political philosophies are appropriate for us in this state, but the price we pay for the cruelties, the wars, the poverty we have created is very high. Could we not aspire to something better?

William Blake saw the world in the eighteenth century as a 'single vision' world, where the basic value is a mechanical and rational one. 'Twofold vision' in his scheme takes into account the clash of opposites and maybe the possibility of their reconciliation. But it is in the four-fold vision that the transcendence of the conflict and reconciliation of opposites takes place. The opposites, the multiplicity, are present in all of the physical world. We constantly need to acknowledge them and go with their flow, as modern chaos and complexity theory understands, for this is the key to spirit. As Blake wrote: "he who sees the infinite in all things sees God. He who sees the ratio only, sees himself only". At present we are stuck with the ratio, the measurement in quantities alone, the need for order and security, but for the spirit we need to wake up. As Genevieve Lloyd points out in her political book *The Man of Reason*, both Blake and Marx, a century apart, recognise that the humanised universe and the fully human individual which are potentially our destiny are not actually our experience in the world. What then has happened to create this disparity? For Blake, the answer lies in man's loss of imagination, whilst for Marx it lies in the alienation of his labour under capitalism. For Lloyd, the problem was in the lack of the feminine. For Jean Liedloff, the fault lay in the way children have been routinely treated in the West. For Bertrand Russell the problem is in human hubris: "in religion and in every deeply serious view of the world and of human destiny, there is an element of submission, a realisation of the limits of human power, which is somewhat missing in the modern world, with its quick material successes and its insolent belief in the boundless possibilities of progress."[14]

The political philosophy that presently dominates the world

springs, I believe, from the partial and dangerous pictures of human nature that have been present in the West for the last four hundred years. Of course, all our pictures are guesses, but it is worth considering alternative images that are older, more inclusive and deeper, less superficial. They are now accessible to us in the literature that has become popular in the last forty years or so. How do we link these new yet very old images of a wider more compassionate social reality that could be waiting to be born?

References

1. Norberg-Hodge, Helena: *Ancient Futures*. Rider Books. 1992 Also see DVD *'The Economics of Happiness'* 2010
2. See Bowes, Pratima: *The Hindu Religious Tradition: a Philosophical Approach*. RKP. 1977. Ch IX
3. Jones, Ken: *The Social Face of Buddhism: an approach to Political and Social Action*. Wisdom Publications, 1989. p33
4. op.cit. p62
5. Capra. Fritjof: *The Tao of Physics*. Fontana/Collins. 1979. p23
6. Smith, Cyprian: *The Way of Paradox: spiritual life as taught by Meister Eckhart*. Darton, Longman and Todd. 1987. p56
7. See Hardy, Jean: *A Psychology with a Soul*. Woodgrange Press. 1996
8. de Chardin, Pierre: *The Divine Milieu*. Collins 1960. p62
9. Avens, Roberts: *The New Gnosis*. Spring Publications 1984. p.109
10. Hoeller, D.: *The Gnostic Jung and the Seven Sermons to the Dead*. Theosophical Publishing House 1982. p75
11. Op.cit. p205
12. Traherne Thomas: *Centuries*. Mowbray. 1975. 29th Meditation
13. Maslow. Abraham: *Towards a Psychology of Being*. Van Nostrand Company 1968. p142
14. Russell, Bertrand: *Mysticism and Logic*. Pelican . 1952 p29

Chapter Fourteen

Politics Conscious and Unconscious: Dark and Golden

"....we need, beyond the political and economic incentives to clean up our land, air and water, to find ways to cultivate an *imaginative* awareness of man's beholden place in the natural order."

Jarold Ramsey, *Reading the Fire.*

In this chapter, I need to bring together some of the disparate strands of the book, which has woven a thread round the theme of political consciousness, political myths and self-fulfilling prophecies over several hundred years, and has argued for a huge change in the political vision we have which needs to be wider, deeper, more inclusive.

Conscious Politics

The story of this book is based around the potentiality of politics, looking for a radical development beyond the traditional and conscious political philosophy and activity of the present day. Political philosophy and practice is concerned with the **ordering** of society and with the power which any social ordering generates, large or small. As such it draws heavily on the left hemisphere of the brain, which has the function of categorising, creating systems and impersonal rulemaking. This is a distinction made by, among others, Iain McGilchrist, a neuroscientist, in his massive recent book entitle *The Master and his Emissary: the divided brain and the making of the Western World*, who argues that the Western World has been essentially created by left brain qualities. The right hand side of the brain, on the other hand, the feeling, synthesising and ultimately deeper side of the brain has a less direct and obvious contribution to make to this political process as it is manifested at present, though immensely strong feeling has gone into the disciplined creation of political philosophy. But it is also with the synthesising element in politics, the right hand hemisphere, that this book is concerned to attend to, towards a more whole vision.

Both Machiavelli and Hobbes saw the imposition of order as their urgent task in times of war: Locke saw it as his function at the beginning of capitalism, to begin to make social and political rules for a totally new social and economic system. Constitutions, laws and governments perform an ordering function in all modern complex societies: it is their conscious rational endeavour to bring both ruling principles into the system, and also to be the mechanism whereby there can be some change within that normal system of order. Modern science and politics of the last four hundred years are a product of this attempt to rule not only society but also to control and understand the natural world which is seen as a human resource, through the rationality of both science and politics.

In Britain there is no written Constitution for this process. As there is a monarchy, ultimate power rests currently and formally in the Queen: according to the vow she makes at the Coronation, this is, by contrast, a religious or spiritual vow. She answers 'yes' to the formal questions posed by the Archbishop of Canterbury, head of the established church when he asks: "Will you to your power cause Law and Justice, in Mercy, to be executed in all your judgments? Will you to the utmost of your power maintain the Laws of God and the true profession of the Gospel?" It is in this religious power and with this promise that she opens each session of Parliament, Commons and Lords and, at least in theory, British political work is spiritually based. It is within such a remit that the political philosophies, parties and practices operate: but this spirituality seems to exert little pressure on the system as a whole.

There is however a strong feeling it this time that the present system has run its useful course. I am writing in the June of 2010, just after the remarkable election of May 6th and its even more riveting aftermath resulting in the coalition government of Conservative and Liberal Democrat parties, under the leadership of David Cameron and Nick Clegg advancing into unchartered seas. It has been becoming clearer ever since the beginning of the twentyfirst century that the British Parliamentary system as it is, is no longer 'fit for purpose'. Using Kuhn's terms in *The Structure of Scientific Revolutions*, 'normal' politics – that which accepts the constitution as it has been built up since the middle ages in this country and more formally since the Act of Union with Scotland in 1707, and discussed in Part One of this book, can no longer do the democratic job that is required in the modern world. We are in a period of what in Kuhnian terms, is called 'revolutionary' politics, where the knowledge base shifts, the old myths and stories die and new ones emerge in their place.

Professor Vernon Bogdanor of Oxford University spelled the situation out last year in his authoritative book *The New British Constitution*. He wrote in the Introduction "We are now in a transition from a system based on parliamentary democracy to one based on the sovereignty of a constitution, albeit a consti-tution that is inchoate, indistinct and still in large part uncod-ified. But we are gradually becoming a constitutional state. And perhaps, peering into the distance, we can perceived, in dim outline, the vision of a state based not on parliamentary sover-eignty, but on a popular sovereignty, upon the sovereignty of the people. Britain would then finally have accepted the full implica-tions of a commitment to democratic government."

I, and millions of others, would of course like to see the changes go further, and incorporate not only a full democracy of humans from every kind of culture, old and new, but one that takes into account all life on earth and the sense of living spirit coursing through all.

Vernon Bogdanor argues that several factors, on the rational, explicit, conscious level of politics, have undermined the present system of British Parliamentary democracy since the end of the Second World War in 1945. These fundamental changes include the setting up of the European Community in the early 1970s and British entry into it in 1973: devolution of the now directly elected Scottish, Welsh and Northern Irish Parliaments in 1998: a directly elected Greater London Authority with its own Mayor, also in 1998 and it is proposed by the 2010 Conservative/Liberal Democrat framework that this should be extended to other major towns: and the proposed introduction of a fairer system of voting for the election of members of these new bodies. There will be changes in the House of Lords which will become an elected body. Government in the future, therefore, will be on a devolved system, involving the European Community, the two new Houses of Parliament, elected Parliaments for Scotland, Wales and Northern Ireland, and enhanced mayoral and local power in towns and countryside.

The Act which Bogdanor sees as the most significant to the changes that are coming, is the Human Rights Act of 1998, which requires government and all public bodies to comply with the provisions of the European Convention on Human Rights: this he sees as the cornerstone of a radically new constitution that is emerging, and "gives us something near to a bill of rights."[1] The ultimate authority is not now the House of Lords but the Court in Strasburg. This formal legislation confirms the principles first worked out in the Europe of 1950 in the Convention of Human Rights, where the intentions were to protect individuals against the horrors millions of people were exposed to in the 1930s-1945 war. This is particularly relevant now that our society has become less homogenous, is far more multicultural and multiracial, and is far more open to different ways and cultures of human life.

Part 1 of this book has traced something of the dialogue over the last four or five hundred years in the political stories that have emerged and been fought out: the conflicts that have arisen at one time were strong enough to result in a Civil War involving the execution of a King: that battle was a deeply spiritual battle between Catholics and Protestants within the Christian faith. Part 2 has reflected on five elements that have been largely omitted within the formal political philosophies: those of gender equality, the wisdom of other older societies in the world, the integrity of the earth and her creatures, the sense of the spiritual in modern times even though it is formally there within our political framework: and the nature of the person particularly the significance of the child. We could indeed relate the structure of a society to that of the person as described in the last chapter. The modern emphasis in politics is on the ego level, on practicality and effectiveness in the material world: this is the rational conscious world. What is lacking is a wider social sense of the Universe and the Earth, which is why we are despoiling her, and a sense of who we are, as individuals in a modern society without any wiser overall concept and conviction. For this wider vision, we need to consider unconscious material and the deeper right-hand part of the brain, because this is our potential.

The dark shadow, conscious and unconscious.

We have only to listen to the news every day to know immediately something of the dark shadow of politics and power as it is manifested in modern life. Just a few obvious facts: that there have been over fifty wars world wide since the end of the Second World War: that one in five of the world's population goes permanently hungry and lives in abject poverty, whilst the richest have abundant wealth and technologies to use beyond previous imagination: that the beautiful planet within we live and the amazing creatures she sustains are treated as though they were a human resource and daily trashed to suit human requirements, destroying species on a large scale as we go. Armaments of ferocious capacity to kill, maim and destroy are regarded as a legitimate item of commerce worldwide and on a huge scale. The practical results of these factors can be seen on television everyday and we are all witnesses. Human beings have existed on this earth for the equivalent time of about 3 minutes at the end of a 24 hour day, and are now **causing** the sixth major extinction of life in her existence. These destructive tendencies have accelerated in the last five hundred years, partly because of the dramatic and continuing rise in population as we have no obvious predators except ourselves, and partly because of the largely aggressive politics and science we have practised in the last five hundred years.

As Ervin Laszlo points out in his very useful book *The Inner Limits of Mankind*, published twenty years ago but still most relevant today, this destruction is not a question of physical resources only, but of the nature of the human psyche. Here he is approaching the unconscious levels of the world problems, the area I was discussing in the second part of this book. He writes: "many world problems involve outer limits, but most of them are due fundamentally to inner limits. There are hardly any world problems that cannot be traced to human agency and which could not be overcome by appropriate changes in human behaviour. The root causes even of physical and ecological problems are the inner constraints of our vision and values. We suffer from a serious case of 'cultural lag'. Living on the threshold of a new age, we squabble among ourselves to acquire or retain the privileges of bygone times. We cast around for innovative ways to satisfy obsolete values. We manage individual crises while heading towards collective catastrophes. We contemplate changing almost anything on earth but ourselves.....coping with mankind's current predicament calls for inner changes, for a human and humanistic revolution mobilising new values and aspirations, backed by new levels of personal commitment and political will."[2] He adds that the problem is one of growth – the growth not of numbers but of mind and spirit.

This is *the* question of human consciousness of course. As Jung pointed out "that which we do not bring to consciousness appears in our lives as fate." It could be argued that the evil we see in the world is a manifestation of unlived life, of unconsciousness, of lack of self knowledge and self awareness, of living out limited stories such as a belief in original sin or in the possibilities of 'possessing' large tracts of the earth which we assume is here for our benefit alone. And I am convinced that a huge element in this skewed and dissatisfied way in which humans often live – Thoreau pointed out that most men live lives of quiet desperation – is due to the way that children are routinely brought up in many societies, so that many, perhaps most, people are in some sense deeply emotionally abused, not fundamentally satisfied.

With the development of depth psychology in the twentieth century, both Freud and Jung named the repressed parts of the human personality: Jung wrote in 1917 in his essay "On the Psychology of the Unconscious," "by shadow I mean the 'negative' side of the personality, the sum of all this unpleasant qualities we like to hide, together with the insufficiently developed functions and the content of the personal unconscious". The 'insufficiently developed functions' refer to those which are omitted and only potential, and to my mind refers to those elements discussed in Part Two of this book – the feminine, the spirit, the sense of the natural world, the satisfied and loving child, wisdom – those elements which we could call the 'golden' unconscious because they are often "not dreamed about in our philosophy".

For Jung, the way through to making the unconscious conscious was to get to know and work with the darkness within oneself. In 1945 he stated "one does not become enlightened by imagining figures of light, but by making the darkness conscious. The latter procedure however is disagreeable and therefore not popular."[3] Jung has taught us an effective way of tackling those inner limits, and gradually depth psychology is giving us a way through to a kinder, wider, deeper way of relating to the world. "We have in all naivety forgotten that beneath our world of reason another lies buried. I do not know what humanity will have to undergo before it admits this."[4] But it seems that only in the recognition and working through of the shadow can the spirit, the true Self, be released.

This darkness is often of course projected onto the Other, as discussed in Part 2 of my book. Sam Keen spells out the story that 'we are good – they are bad'.

We are innocent	They are guilty
We tell the truth – inform	They lie – use progaganda
We only defend ourselves	They are aggressors
We have a defence dept.	They have a war dept.
Our missiles and weapons are designed to deter	Their weapons are for first strike

Given that framework, that projection, and believing that people – especially men – are intrinsically warlike, no wonder we have wars. Believing that people are essentially simple, describable with one adjective – economic man, rational man, warlike man – is not true. People are complex, full of contradictions, each essentially unique and our philosophy and stories must start from there.

The golden shadow, conscious and unconscious
Gerard Manley Hopkins' poem at the beginning of Chapter Twelve maintains that every creature comes to fulfil its own unique potential – "What I do is me: for that I came". Surely the same thing may be true of the human race: "now we see through a glass darkly......" but we search for what we truly are, not only

as persons but also as a species. There is the haunting sense that both I as an individual, and the human race itself, could become far greater, could fill out with generosity nearer to our potential. There was in the Middle Ages, that much more religious age, a sin known as 'accidie': the sin of not fulfilling your potential. That potential surely involves a relationship with everything that is, a sense that everything is interconnected, and that you can grow into that relationship of spirit.

There have been various studies lately of the growth of a cultural response worldwide to the kind of greedy modern society which presently pervades the world: this response is one springing from a resistance to the dominant political and economic values of the West, and the active search for a different, more compassionate and kindly way of life for all creatures. Paul Hawken recently produced a thought-provoking study of active and world wide movements which are criticising and trying to change the inequalities, warlike and cruel behaviour and destruction of nature currently commonly practised, calling his book *Blessed Unrest.* These movements and organisations are of course individually entirely intentional but in their numbers seem to be an instinctive, imaginative and unconscious world-wide phenomenon. Hawken has come to the conclusion that "this is the largest social movement of all human history"[5] dedicated to change. "What I see", he writes in 2007, "are ordinary and some not-so-ordinary individuals willing to confront despair, power, and incalculable odds in an attempt to restore some semblance of grace, justice, and beauty to this world". He numbers over one million organisations as the extent of the protest against the injustice and violence of the day, which would involve many millions of people perhaps up to a billion, and growing. The organisations would include Amnesty, the World Wildlife Fund, Oxfam, Human Rights and Ecological movements, Quaker organisations against the Arms Trade and so on, the list of which covers the last third of his book.

His book is consistent with several other studies that have

been published in the last few years. Several of these are to do with the growth of spiritual awareness in the western world. This awareness has emerged at various times over the last 150 years, there was a great surge of awareness in the Arts and in new religions based upon Eastern thought, particularly Buddhism, at the end of the nineteenth century which was halted by the First World War. It included the Arts and Crafts Movement, Art Nouveau, the work inspired by William Morris and the beginnings of Theosophy. Then at the end of the 1960s and well into the seventies, a whole alternative, green, feminist, flower-power and very musical movement began in both Europe and America and involved a whole generation of alternative thinking which has lasted to this day. Inspiration from these alternative movements, the growing inspiration from indigenous societies and their values through travel particularly by young people, and a radical disenchantment with capitalism, especially the neoliberalism of the 1980s and onwards, has joined with ever more concerned ecologist movements aware of the dramatic and dangerous human impact upon the earth.

One very interesting book published in 2004 is by David Tacey about the growth of contemporary spirituality in young people in Australia. He writes that this is due to "our secular society realising that it has been running on empty, and has to restore itself at a deep, primal source which is beyond humanity and yet paradoxically at the very core of our experience."[6] Spirituality, unlike formal religion, is available to all who search for a greater depth in life, and who begin to look for the sacred and the interconnections of life everywhere. He writes that this is "a direct political and philosophical challenge to traditional notions of sacredness and the holy,"[7] and this allows people who experience a sense of the whole to see that they are more than the egos, their personalities, and can live in this world, as Thomas Berry puts it, not as in a collection of objects but "as a communion of subjects". Tacey uses the reflections of his students at Monash University,

Melbourne, to create his book, and comments that he continues to be impressed by the vitality and strength of youth spirituality which is flourishing worldwide – and yet of course it is not countable as there is no membership.

Healing

I am not a mechanism, an assembly of various sections.

And it is not because the mechanism is working wrongly,
    that I am ill

I am ill because of the wounds to the soul, to the deep
    emotional self

and the wounds to the soul take a long, long time, only
    time can help

and patience, and a certain difficult repentance,

long, difficult repentance, realisation of life's mistake,
    and the freeing oneself

from the endless repetitions of the mistake

which mankind at large has chosen to sanctify.

D.H. Lawrence

References

1. Bogdanor, Vernon: *The New British Constitution.* Oxford and Portland, Oregon. 2009. p63
2. Lazslo, Ervin: *The Inner Limits of Mankind.*One World 1989. pp 26/7
3. Zweig, Connie & Abrams, Jeremiah, (eds.): *Meeting the Shadow.*TarcherPutnam/Penguin. 1990
4. op.cit. pXXIII
5. Hawken, Paul: *Blessed Unrest.*Viking. 2007.p4
6. Tacey, David: *The Spirituality Revolution, the emergence of contemporary spirituality*, Brunner-Routledge, 2004. p1
7. op.cit. p5.

Chapter Fifteen

Thinking about a Wiser Politics

Jerusalem

I will not cease from Mental Fight,
Nor will my Sword sleep in my hand,
Till we have built Jerusalem
In England's green and pleasant land.

William Blake (1757-1827).

* * *

The Swing

Between the conscious and the unconscious, the mind has put
up a swing:
all earth creatures, even the supernovas, sway between these
two trees,
and it never winds down.

Angels, animals, humans, insects by the million, also the
wheeling sun and Moon;
Ages go by, and it goes on.

Everything is swinging: heaven, earth, water, fire,
and the secret one slowly growing a body.
Kabir saw that for fifteen seconds, and it made him a servant
for life.

Kabir (15th century)

Our present politics of the last 500 years rest on a particular view of human nature – that of the individual archetypal man in action, vigorous, changing the world. Machiavelli's Prince is a powerful leader of a wealthy Italian city state, who must learn the devious skills essential to a successful ruler. Hobbes' man is essentially warlike and controlling, both in the state and in the family. Locke's man digs the earth and in doing so becomes the possessor of his plot large or small. Even Blake's man in the poem above has sword in hand, and also his bow and chariots of fire, to build the alternative iconic city in England's 'green and pleasant land'. This male figure has dominated our modern world.

Kabir, however, an Indian of the fourteenth century, has a different vision of the potential of all life. It is infinitely wide, imagining the whole universe, conscious and unconscious, including all creatures. The universe is pregnant and everything is interconnected. Instead of the person being the initiator, she or he needs to perceive and respond to the miracle in which we already exist. For me, this is an image close to the one I am searching for in this book. The male figure is not denied, but he is just part of everything else – the female is just as significant, the spirit runs through all things, the earth and indeed the whole universe is the container of all activity: humans, far from being in control, are held within an infinitely greater whole.

* * *

There is and has possibly always been a human sense that both individuals and the human race have a potential which is yearned for but which is not yet fulfilled. We find an amazing world, intelligent, powerful and beautiful beyond our capacity to measure or appreciate, and humans write their stories over it even though these must be paltry tales compared with the original. How can we begin to perceive a much wider vision?

First we have to look again and far more critically at what stories we presently accept and live out; this has been the subject of the first part of this book. Some human stories are known as political philosophies, and we have in Europe been developing a political dialogue which has penetrated round the world, mostly though the power of Empire: the dialogue has become global. But there is an urgent sense that these old stories are not enough, and indeed several are positively destructive. We search for alternatives. Even parochially in the present political scene in England we have suffered a 'New Labour' pretty disastrously in the last ten years, and are at present in search of a 'New Politics' altogether in the Conservative/ Liberal Democrat Alliance. There is a strong sense that the old definitions and stories are now anachronistic, and that democracy itself needs refreshing, becoming more fit for what will be the extraordinary challenges of the twenty-first century.

In Britain, our present political parties, Conservative, Liberal, Labour in Britain today are all defined by their relationship to Capitalism and Individualism, as was Communism. R.H.Tawney's study of *Religion and the Rise of Capitalism* traces the decline of the medieval sin of Avarice and its accompanying practice of Usury – lending money in exchange for the payment of Interest - which happened around the sixteenth century. He lists the medieval arguments against these practices: "to take usury is contrary to Scripture; it is contrary to Aristotle; it is contrary to nature, for it is to live without labour; it is to sell time, which belongs to God, for the advantage of wicked men...."[1] But by the seventeenth century, borrowing money for interest and accumulating capital had ignored these prohibitions and become legalised. By then 'usury' was a necessary tool for the mastery of mankind over nature – and it was from nature's resources that most of the profit was won. Much of the profits went into the endless wars that have lasted to this day. Tawney, no supporter of capitalism of course, sums up his criticism at the end of his study by writing that capitalism "consists in the assumption ......that the attainment of material riches is the supreme object of human endeavour, and the final criterion of human success."[2] This economic imperative is widely accepted today, and is a major dominating myth that needs to be severely questioned and hopefully demolished. We must re-categorise the human economic relationship to the earth and all her creatures.

The Conservative thrust is to accept the economic system, which has now spread globally, and the individualism and the propensity for war that goes with it. As Margaret Thatcher announced so firmly: "there is no such thing as Society" and she was quickly into the Falklands war. The Liberal take on capitalism is to accept it, especially in its possessive individualism, its propensity for Free Trade, and its guarding of privacy, including the freedom of individual consciousness. "A man can do what he likes so long as he doesn't interfere with his neighbour" – though now of course we see it's quite difficult to do almost anything without interfering with others. The Socialist criticizes some of the basic tenets of the Capitalist system, and fights for greater equality within the system: nowadays most socialists would argue against Neoliberalism, but don't generally question the basis of capitalism as the economic basis of society. This was particularly true of New Labour in the 1997-2010 government. In America, it is virtually regarded as unpatriotic to question the basis of Capitalism, and the wealth it brings, and it is this American version that has been so attractive to the modernizing countries in the rest of the world. This version could be summed up by a present witticism quoted recently by the BBC World Service that "making a profit is Nature's way of telling you you're a useful part of the Universe!" How ridiculous! It is a way of connecting Cosmos, Polis and Psyche which could hardly be more destructive as most profit is directly taken from the resources of the earth!

Our modern politics are also increasingly linked in to the

findings of modern Science which is heavily subsidized by the modern State. Modern science and modern politics, as we have traced in the book, emerged together with modern economics to form the powerful yet unsustainable and in many ways immoral world we have today. All these stories are myths we urgently need to question, and see from a wider, and a wiser, perspective.

* * *

The political world is now much more complex than the map of nation states would lead us to believe. The number of nations is increasing all the time to reach near the 200 mark. At the same time global alliances, many of them hardened into legislation, group nations into alliances both financial and political. There is, as Bogdanor pointed out, also a growing human rights legislation. This now needs extending into those areas presently omitted in our present political philosophy, particularly in relation to the earth and her creatures. Thomas Berry has written a very powerful Introduction to Cormac Cullinan's *Wild Law: A Manifesto for Earth Justice*, a book that is advocating the extention of the rights legislation to the land and to all species where appropriate. We would not now be destroying the earth if, together, we loved her: but as we don't seem to love her enough, we need legislation to stop the terrible contraventions we commit in relation to the natural world – and to our own souls.

Berry, an American, comments on the human-centred constitutions and modes of thought we live by in the West. "From the beginning", he writes "the American Constitution was clearly a document framed for the advancement of the human with no significant referent to any other power in heaven or on Earth.....humans had become self-validating, both as individuals and as a political community. This self-validation was invented and sustained by the union of the commercial-entrepreneurial powers with the legal judicial powers to sustain the assault on the natural world". Berry goes on to say:-

"It would be appropriate if the prologue to any (new) founding Constitution enacted by humans would state in its opening lines a clear recognition that our own human existence and well-being are dependent on the well-being of the larger Earth Community out of which we were born and upon which we depend for our continued survival. This…might be followed by a statement that care of this larger Earth Community is a primary obligation of the nation being founded."[3] And it has become even more obvious than this in our globally interconnected world, because it becomes clearer and clearer that no nation now can do as it likes without interfering with its many neighbours – indeed all the rest of the living world. **Everything is interconnected**, and that is the primary perception upon which a wiser politics must be founded.

This is where the disciplines, now separated, must come together – politics, economics, biology, paleontology, psychology, spirituality, science, geography, music and arts. We have learned to think in divisions, as Dickens' Mr Gradgrind indicated two centuries ago. We must no longer do so, and increasing knowledge in all areas will surely soon lead to new paradigms of understanding and action.

This is how Richard Fortey in his book *Life: A Natural History of the first Four Billion Years of Life on Earth* puts it:

"What is abundantly clear is that *all* life – from bacterium to elephant – shares common characteristics at the level of molecules. There is a common thread that runs through the whole of biological existence……These molecules run through life in the same way as a musical theme runs through the last movement of Brahms's Fourth Symphony. There is a set of variations which superficially sound very different but which are underpinned by a deeper similarity that binds the whole. The beauty of the structure depends on the individuality of the passing music, and also on the coherence of the construction. The vital spark from inanimate matter to animate earth happened once and only once, and all living existence depends upon that moment. We are one with bacteria that lives in hot springs, parasitic barnacles, vampire bats and cauliflowers. We all share a common ancestor."[4]

We **have** to live out these truths in the twenty first century, to survive.

* * *

What would politics look like if we started from this infinitely wider vision? I would like to begin to spell out some of the implications:-

i.   If we had a more whole view of the human person as female as well as male, as ensouled when born, as containing all the opposites found in nature, as needing meaning as well as food and shelter, we would be obliged to:-

- ensure that **all** babies and children were physically and emotionally cared for, and time given to adults to fulfil this primary function of love
- provide an education that enabled children and adults to find their own individual potential through life
- have an education based on the awareness of the whole universe, the earth, and the human space within this sacred environment

To care appropriately for offspring is the task of all species on the planet. We do not presently do this at all adequately.

ii.   Outgrow wars and the making of armaments, particularly land-mines. Stop trying to solve problems in the mode of three-year-old children, and become truly adult. Abolish the arms-trade, and minimize the military. This would save a lot of money.

iii. Value biodiversity in all species, including our own, and take all measures to provide the means for all to flourish. Consider the concept of 'the Other' as considered in Ryszard Kapuschinski's work.[5] The 'Other' is apparent in many ways in our multicultural, multispecies universe.

iv.   Work towards far greater equality within human populations, on the Swedish model where no person earns more than x10 (or less) in relation to others.

v.   Abolish the myth of the 'owning' of land. Re-establish forests.

vi.   Develop a World Community and a consciousness of world citizenship: and also develop Locality, and maximum participation at that level for all. A greater sense of place and localization gives a security to all. Keep goods circulating in a limited way: this builds up community and a feeling for one's own area.

vii. Question modern farming practices, working towards the minimum eating of meat and fish. No more cattle and sheep kept for human consumption: we should not raise millions of cows and pigs for the sole purpose of slaughtering them to provide meat for our table.

viii. Develop alternative energy resources to fossil fuels.

ix. Political Parties, if they continued, would be based not on their relationship to an increasingly irrelevant capitalism but to other issues as they arose.

x.   Size of world population of humans would always be a potent issue as we have no other predators than ourselves.

xi. Develop a means of joint control of the implications of new and existing technologies, as there is only one planet. Not all new inventions should be developed.

xii. Encourage self-sufficiency at the local level, following the model of the Transition Towns movement, which is now spreading round the planet. Work at all levels towards a simpler life-style.

xiii. Work towards a more realistic understanding of the human place on earth, taking into account the relationship of Universe, individual being and societies of all living beings.

xiv. Develop an economic system which is not antagonistic to these principles. Re-examine the concept of usury, lending money for interest, which is the basis of capitalism: consider whether the 'profit' basically comes from using more of the earth's resources.

These points and many others are discussed in two excellent books by Ervin Lazslo. The first, published in 1989, is called *The Inner Limits of Mankind*. The key to this book is summed up in his words on the back cover: "It is forgotten that not our world, but we human beings are the cause of our problems, and that only by redesigning our thinking and acting, not the world around us, can we solve them." This of course has been the key to this present book of mine. It is a shift of consciousness that is required throughout the globe, but particularly in the west. This point was made particularly forcefully by Carl Jung in discussing his psychotherapeutic work: "All the greatest and most important problems of life are fundamentally insoluble…They can never be solved but only outgrown. This 'outgrowing' proved on further investigation to require a new level of consciousness. Some higher or wider interest appeared on the patient's horizon, and through this broadening of his or her outlook the insoluble problem lost its urgency. It was not solved logically in its own terms but faded when confronted with a new and stronger life urge."[6] Lazslo's book is about that leap into a new realization, when the struggles of the present can be suddenly seen from a new place.

That place may be already in sight, partly because of the massive fear of violence and destruction we have, examples of which we constantly see on television. We see some of the evidence for the reality of climate change before our eyes in the shrinking of the icecaps, and the fears of people living on small vulnerable islands: we learn vividly of our own destructiveness in the massive gushing of oil in the Mexican Seas, onto the coasts of Louisiana and in the terrible coating of pelicans in the oil, as well as the agony of people in the disappearance of their familiar habitat. Though there is enormous devoted work of environmentalists, both individual lovers of the earth caring for land and animals, and the devoted work of such organisations as the World Wildlife Trust or Greenpeace, we hear of species becoming extinct and see on film the uniqueness of those still just remaining. And we begin to know of the predictions that these huge environmental changes caused by our use of the world's resources over the last few hundred years, may very well mean, according to James Lovelock and many others, that the human population may be decimated in the next hundred years from the 6-7 billion people we have today and the 9 billion we are expecting by mid-century, down to 1 billion in only a hundred years time though the cataclysmic forces we seem to be unleashing. We often see people starving on television.

These fears are at last breaking through to more of us – and also leading to a new resolve, as time seems to be so short. Lazslo's most recent book was published in 2009 and looks to 2012 as the year in which a new realization could spread world wide. The book is called *Worldshift 2012: Making Green Business, New Politics & Higher Consciousness Work Together.* It is consistent with Lester Brown's *Plan B: Mobilising to Save Civilisation,* published in 2008, and one of an annual authoritative series published by the Earth Policy Institute, and equally, and with more detail, offering plans for survival in the long run on the planet.

Lazslo once again emphasizes how necessary the importance of a world vision is for individuals and societies. "Possessing the human kind of consciousness is a unique privilege, and it confers a unique responsibility. It allows us to rediscover ourselves in the cosmic order of things, and it gives us the moral obligation to do so. When we perceive our place in the universe we come to know our role and our mission: to be truly one with the world of which we are an intrinsic part."[7] This consciousness requires imagination and a width of mind seen only patchily, though increasingly, today.

* * *

Politics itself still has to be seen alongside economic capitalism: indeed world national and local politics will be the places in which the conflict will be played out between the powerful forces of the present capitalist system and the growing protests against the threats this world view poses, will be played out. Capitalism represents the lefthand side of the brain – the rational, ordering, controlling system which should be the servant and has come to seem like the master. The righthand side of the brain is the larger organ and represent synthesis, imagination, intuition and the greater interplay of the two is what is essential at this point in human history.

Thomas Berry in his classic book *The Great Work* sums up the difference between the two perspectives: "to the one group the human is considered primary in terms of reality and value while the larger, more integral Earth community is a secondary consideration. In the other group the integral Earth community (including the human) is seen as primary while human wellbeing is itself seen as derivative. The one insists that the natural life systems must adapt primarily to human purposes. The other insists that the human must adapt to the priority of natural life systems. Ultimately there must be a mutual adaptation of the human and natural life systems."[8]

In England we have our first Green Party Member of Parliament (though the Green party themselves keep referring to the earth as "the environment" as though it were the human environment only, and not fully alive in its own right). But we have already done so much harm, and the commercial-industrial order is so powerful and pervasive in government , commerce, the medical profession, education and throughout modern life as it spreads over the planet. The petroleum based economy has to come to an end, but the wealthy nations try their utmost to substitute alternatives for that energy, rather than working towards a simpler life-style. There is development however, often implemented with great enthusiasm, in organic farming and gardening, in the redesigning of some houses, in more thoughtful use of extravagant ways of travelling; groups all over the world are working towards a different vision as the sheer destructiveness and thoughtlessness of our present ways of living become clearer. Countries are being forced to economise themselves because of the greedy practices of banks. High incomes are being examined more, and banking practices more regulated. Sustainable development becomes widespread, with varied kinds of meaning. Many important and urgent books are written and films produced.

A truly wiser politics goes deeper. It requires a cultural shift amongst many people and nations, a particularly big shift amongst the wealthiest politicians and people of power, and feeling of recognition by the billions who have lived, generation after generation, down this long cul-de-sac of a story that is based on fear and competition. The present stories are leading us into more and more of a nightmare.

We need to understand and grow into a bigger change of mind, heart and soul that would make for a truly wiser politics: a shift that that would call for a politics that is not solely managerial and short term, but is philosophically based and deeply felt. We need to understand and question the assumptions of the human attempt to control the earth and to embrace another kinder, more imaginative and fulfilling story, nearer to our personal, social and spiritual potential, so beginning to actually appreciate who we are as persons and acknowledge this amazing place we inhabit.

References

1. Tawney, R.H.: *Religion and the Rise of Capitalism*. Penguin 1984.p55
2. op.cit. p280
3. Cullinan, Cormac: *Wild Law, A Manifesto for Earth justice*. Green Books. 2003.Foreword by Berry p13
4. Fortey, Richard: *Life: an Unauthorised Biography. A Natural History of the first 4,000,000,000 years of Life on Earth*. Harper Perennial. 1998. pp39-40
5. Kapuschinski, Ryszard : *The Other*. Verso.2006
6. Jung, Carl, in Jacobi, Jolande, (ed.): *C.G. Jung. Psychological reflections. A New Anthology of his writings*. New York. p304.
7. Laszlo, Ervin: *Worldshift 2012: Making Green Business, New Politics and Higher Consciousness Work Together*. Inner Traditions 2009. p93
8. Thomas Berry: *The Great Work*. Bell Tower. New York. 1999 p108

God's Grandeur

The world is charged with the grandeur of God.
It will flame out, like shining from shook foil;
It gathers to a greatness, like the ooze of oil
Crushed. Why do men then now not reek his rod?
Generations have trod, have trod, have trod;
 And all is seared with trade; bleared, smeared with toil;
 And wears man's smudge, and shares man's smell: the soil
Is bare now, nor can foot feel, being shod.

And, for all this, nature is never spent;
    There lives the dearest freshness deep down things;
And though the last lights off the black West went
    Oh, morning, at the brown brink eastward, springs –
Because the Holy Ghost over the bent
 World brood s with warm beast, and with ah! bright wings.

Gerard Manley Hopkins (1844-1889)

Bibliography

Anderson, J.K: *Xenophon*. Duckworth.1974

Aries, P: *Centuries of Childhood*. Penguin. 1986

Armstrong, K: *A Short History of Myth*. Canongate.2005

Avens, R: *The New Gnosis*. Spring Publications.1984

Avery, C & Colebrook, M: *The Green Mantle of Romanticism* Greenspirit Press. 2008

Bateson G: *Mind and Nature:* Flamingo. 1979

Beer, G: *Darwin's Plots:* Ark 1983

Belotti, E.G: *Little Girls.* Writers and Readers Cooperative. 1975

Berger, J: *Ways of Seeing.* BBC & Penguin. 1979

Berger, P: *The Social Construction of Reality. 1977*

Berlin, I: *The Roots of Romanticism.* Princetown Univ. 2001 *Against the Current* Pimlico 1997

Berman, M: *The Reenchantment of the World.* Bantam 1984

Berry, T: *The Great Work; our Way into the Future.* Bell Tower. 1999

Blackwell, T, Seabrook J: *The Politics of Hope:* Faber & Faber. 1988

Bly, R: *A Little Book on the Human Shadow:* Harper & Row. 1988

Bogdanor, V: *The New British Constitution.* Oxford and Portland. 2009

Bohm, D: *Wholeness and the Implicate Order.* RKP. 1980

Bottomore, T.B. & Rubel, M. (eds.)

Bowes, P : *The Hindu Religious Tradition: A Philosophic Approach* RKP. 1977

Bowler, P : *Evolution: the History of an Idea.* Univ. of California Press. 1984

Brailsford, H.N : *The Levellers and the English Revolution.* ed Christopher Hill. Spokesman 1973

Briggs, J & Peat, D: *Seven Life Lessons of Chaos.* HarperPerennial. 1999

Brindle, S: *To Learn a New Song.* Australia Yearly Meeting. Society of Friends (Quakers). 2000

Burke, E: *Reflections on the Revolution in France.* 1790 *The Appeal from the New to Old Whigs.* 1791

Burrow, J.W. *Evolution and Society.* Cambridge U.P. 1982

Butler, E. *Hayek:* Temple Smith. 1983

Campbell, J: *Pathways to Bliss.* New World Library. 2004 *The Inner Reaches of Outer Space.* Harper & Row 1988 *Myths to Live By.* Condor 1972

Capra, F: *The Tao of Physics.* Fontana 1979 *The Turning Point.* Wildwood.1982

Carson, R: *Silent Spring.* Houghton Mifflin Company. 1962

Cassirer, E: *The Individual and the Cosmos in Renaissance Philosophy.* Univ. Pennsylvania Press. 1983

Chardin, Pierre de: *Le Milieu Divin.* Collins 1960

Chenu, M-D: *Man and Society in the Twelfth Century.* Univ. Toronto Press. 1997

Clements, H: *Alfred Russel Wallace.* Hutchinson. 1983

Coole, D: *Women in Political Theory.* Wheatsheaf 1988

Cooper, J.C: *Yin and Yang: the Taoist harmony of opposites.* Aquarian Press. 1981

Cullinan, C: *Wild Law: a Manifesto for Earth Justice.* Green Books 2003

Darwin, C: *The Origin of Species.* Penguin 1968

Darwin, F. (ed): *The Autobiography of Charles Darwin.* Dover Publications. 1958

Easlea, B: *Witch-hunting, Magic and the New Philosophy.* Harvester. 1980

Ehrenfeld, D: *The Arrogance of humanism.* Oxford U.P. 1978

Eisler, R: *The Chalice and the Blade.* Harper and Row. 1987

Eiseley, L: *The Unexpected Universe.* Harvester. 1969

Eliade, M: *The Myth of the Eternal Return.* Princeton U.P. 1974

Ellenberger, H: *The Discovery of the Unconscious.* Basic. 1970

Erikson, C: *The Medieval Vision.* Oxford U.P. 1976

Fortey, R: *Life: An Unauthorised Biography. A natural history of the first 4,000,000,000 years of Life on Earth.* Flamingo.1998

Fox, M: *Original Blessing.* Bear &Co. 1983 *Western Spirituality.* Bear 1981

Freire, P: *Pedogogy of the Oppressed.* Penguin 1972

Fromm, E: *Fear of Freedom.* Routledge. 1963 *The Anatomy of Human Destructiveness.* Penguin 1973

Gilbert, Kevin: *Black from the Edge.* Hyland House. 1994

Griffiths, B: *The Marriage of East and West.* Collins. 1972 *A New Vision of Reality.* Collins 1989

Grimshaw, J: *Feminist Philosophers.* Wheatsheaf Books. 1986

Grimsley, R: *Jean-Jacques Rousseau.* Harvester 1986

Haddock, B: *Vico's Political Thought.* Harvester 1983

Hall, J: *Rousseau: an Introduction to his Political Philosophy.* Macmillan. 1973

Hampton, C. (ed): *A Radical Reader.* Penguin. 1984

Harding, S: *Animate Earth: Science, Intuition and Gaia.* Green Books. 2006

Hardy, J: *A Psychology with a Soul.* Woodgrange Press 1996 *There is Another World but it is This One.* Quaker Universalist Group. 1988 reprints.

Hausheer, R: *Introduction*, in Berlin's *Against the Current.* op.cit

Hawken, P: *Blessed Unrest.* Viking. 2007

Hayek, F: *The Road to Serfdom.* RKP. 1944

Heilbrun, C: *Towards Androgeny.* Gollancz. 1973

Heinberg, R: *Memories and Visions of Paradise.* The Aquarian Press. 1990

Hewetson, J: *Introductory Essay, Mutual Aid and Social Evolution* to Kropotkin's *Mutual Aid.* op.cit.

Hobbes, T: *Leviathan.* Penguin. 1968

Hoeller, S: *The Gnostic Jung and the Seven Sermons to the Dead.* Theosophical Publishing House. 1982

Huxley, A: *The Perennial Philosophy.* Chatto & Windus. 1980

Jacobi, J (ed.): *C.G. Jung. Psychological Reflections, A New Anthology of his writings.* New York

Jacobson, N: *Pride and Solace: the functions and limitations of political theory.* Methuen. 1978

Jones, K: *The Social Face of Buddhism: an approach to social and political action.* Wisdom Publications. 1989

Jung, C.G: *The Secret of the Golden Flower* RKP 1979 *Modern Man in search of a Soul* RKP. 1981 *The Archetypes and the Collective Unconscious.* Routledge 2008

Kapuschinski, R: *The Other.* Verso 1906

Kauffman, S: *Reinventing the Sacred.* Perseus Books Group. 2008

Keen, S: *The Enemy Maker.* In Zweig C. & Abrams J: *Meeting the Shadow: op.cit.*

Kelly, J.N.D: *Early Christian Doctrines.* A&C Black. 1985

Kennedy, E & Mendus, S (eds): *Women in Western Political Philosophy,* Wheatsheaf. 1987

Kropotkin, P: *Mutual Aid.* Freedom Press. 1987

Kuhn, T: *The Structure of Scientific Revolutions.* Univ.Chicago 1973

Laszlo, E: *The Inner Limits of Mankind.* Oneworld 1989 *Science and the Reenchantment of the Universe* Inner Traditions. Vermont. 2006 *Worldshift 2012: Making Green Business, New Politics and Higher Consciousness Work Together.* Inner Traditions. 2009

Lear, L: *Rachel Carson.* Penguin Press. 1997

Liedloff, J: *The Continuum Concept.* Penguin 1986

Lindsay J: *William Blake.* Constable. 1978

Lloyd, G: *The Man of Reason: 'male' and 'female' in Western Philosophy.* Methuen 1984

Lovejoy, A: *The Great Chain of Being.* Harvard Univ.Press. 1978

Lovelock, J: *The Ages of Gaia.* Oxford Univ. Press. 1988

Maslow, A: *The Furthest Reaches of Human Nature.* Penguin 1978

Macfarlane, A: *The Origins of English Individualism.* Blackwell 1978

McGilchrist, I: *The Master and his Emissary: the divided brain and the making of the Western World.* Yale Univ. Press. 2009

McGregor, R.K: *A Wider View of the Universe. Henry Thoreau's study of Nature.* Univ. of Illinois 1997

MacKenzie, N & J: *The First Fabians.* Quartet. 1979

McLellan, D: *Karl Marx: Selected Writings.* Oxford U.P. 1977

MacPherson C: *The Political Theory of Possessive Individualism.* Oxford Univ Press. 1962 *Property.* Blackwell. 1978

Malthus, T: *An Essay on the Principle of Population.* Oxford Univ. Press. 2008

Maslow, A: *Towards a Psychology of Being.* Van Nostrand Company. 1968

Mason, J: *The Indispensible Rousseau.* Quartet Books. 1979

de Mause, L: *The History of Childhood: the untold story of child abuse.* Bellew Publications. 1991

Mendoza, R: *The Acentric Universe: Giordano Bruno's Prelude to Contemporary Cosmology.* Element. 1995

Merchant, C: *The Death of Nature.* Wildwood. 1980

Mill J.S.: *Three Essays: On Liberty: Representative Government: The Subjection of Women.* Oxford U.P. 1975

Miller, A: *For Your Own Good: hidden cruelty in childhood and the roots of violence.* Virago 1987 *Thou Shalt Not Be Aware.* Pluto Press. 1985

Moacanin, R: *Jung's Psychology and Tibetan Buddhism.* Wisdom 1962

Nesfield-Cookson,B: *William Blake: prophet of universal brotherhood.* Crucible. 1987

Neumann, E: *The Origin and History of Consciousness.* RKP 1954

Norberg-Hodge, H: *Ancient Futures.* Rider Books. 1992

O'Gorman, F: *Edmund Burke: his Political Philosophy.* 2004

Paine, T: *Common Sense:* Penguin 1983

Patten, C: *The Tory Case.* Longman 1983

Phipps, J-F: *The Politics of Inner Experience.* Green Print. 1990

Pinto-Duschinsky, M: *The Political Thought of Lord Salisbury.*

Pitkin, H: *Fortune is a Woman: Gender and Politics in the Thought of Niccolo Machiavelli.* Univ. of California Press. 1984

de Quincey, C: *Radical Knowing: Understanding Consciousness through Relationship.* Park Street Press. Vermont. 2005

Raby, P: *Alfred Russel Wallace, A Life.* Chatto & Windus. 2001

Raine, K: *Defending Ancient Springs.* Golgonooza Press. 1985

Rendall, J: *The Origins of Modern Feminism*. Macmillan 1985

Rousseau, J-J: *The Social Contract and Other Discourses*. Dent 1973. *On Inequality. Emile.*

Roszak, T: *The Voice of the Earth*. Touchstone Books.1993

Russell, B: *A Free Man's Worship*. Portland, Maine. 1923 *Mysticism and Logic*. Pelican .1952

Sale, Kirkpatrick: *The Conquest of Paradise: Christopher Columbus and the Columbian Legacy*. Hodder & Stoughton 1991

Sardar, Z, Nandy A, & Wyn, D.M: *Barbaric Others*. Pluto Press. 1993

Smith, C: *The Way of Paradox: spiritual life as taught by Meister Eckhart*. Darton, Longman and Todd.1987

Smith, L.T: *Decolonising Mythologies*. Zed Books. 2008

Singer, J: *Androgeny*. RKP 1977

Stein, M: *Jung's Map of the Soul*. Open Court. 1998

Swimme, B. & Berry, T: *The Universe Story*. HarperSanFrancisco. 1992

Tacey, David: *The Spirituality Revolution: the emergence of contemporary spirituality*. Brunner-Routledge, 2004

Tarnas, R: *Cosmos and Psyche*. Viking. 2006

Tawney, R.H.: *Religion and the Rise of Capitalism*. Penguin 1984

Taylor, A: *Visions of Harmony: a study of nineteenth century millenarianism*. Clarendon Press. 1987

Taylor, S: *The Fall*. O-Books. 2005

Thoreau, H:*Walden*. Signet Books 1949

Traherne, T: *Centuries*. Mowbray. 1975

Tsuzuki, C: *Edward Carpenter 1844-1929. Prophet of Human Fellowship*. Cambridge U.P. 1980

Watts, A: *The Wisdom of Insecurity*. Rider 1974

Weber, M: *The Protestant Ethic and the Spirit of Capitalism*. Unwin Books. 1976

Willey, B: *The Seventeenth Century Background*. Ark. 1986

Whyte, L.L: *The Unconscious before Freud*. Julian Friedman. 1978

Wood, N: *The Politics of Locke's Philosophy*. Univ. California Press.

1983

Young, L: *The Unfinished Universe.* Simon & Schuster. 1986

Zweig, C & Abrams, J (eds.): *Meeting the Shadow: The Hidden Power of the Dark Side of Human Nature.* Jeremy Tarcher. 1990

Index of Names, social and political terms, and Events

Names have capital letters: social movements and events are in small case

BOOKS

O is a symbol of the world, of oneness and unity. In different cultures it also means the "eye," symbolizing knowledge and insight. We aim to publish books that are accessible, constructive and that challenge accepted opinion, both that of academia and the "moral majority."

Our books are available in all good English language bookstores worldwide. If you don't see the book on the shelves ask the bookstore to order it for you, quoting the ISBN number and title. Alternatively you can order online (all major online retail sites carry our titles) or contact the distributor in the relevant country, listed on the copyright page.

See our website **www.o-books.net** for a full list of over 500 titles, growing by 100 a year.

And tune in to myspiritradio.com for our book review radio show, hosted by June-Elleni Laine, where you can listen to the authors discussing their books.

MySpiritRadio